The Bible On Christian Unity

The Bible

on

Christian

Unity

by J. S. LESCRAUWAET

Translated by N. D. SMITH

ST. NORBERT ABBEY PRESS
De Pere, Wisconsin
U. S. A.
1965

Biblical quotations are from the Revised Standard Version of the Bible, copyrighted 1946 and 1952 by the Division of Christian Education, National Council of Churches, and used by permission.

Nihil obstat:

Samuel D. Jadin, O. Praem.
Censor deputatus
July 23, 1965

Imprimatur:

†Stanislaus V. Bona, D.D.
Bishop of Green Bay
August 6, 1965

The *Nihil obstat* and *Imprimatur* are a declaration that a book or pamphlet is considered free from doctrinal or moral error. It is not implied that those who have granted the *Nihil obstat* and *Imprimatur* agree with the contents, opinions or statements expressed.

Originally published as
De Bijbel over de Christelijke Eenheid
Roermond and Maaseik, J. J. Romen & Zonen, 1961

Library of Congress catalogue card number: 65 - 22863

Printed in the United States of America
ST. NORBERT ABBEY PRESS
De Pere, Wisconsin

CONTENTS

FOREWORD

Where better should divided Christians seek counsel, in their attempts to find a solution to the scandal of separation, than in the Book of the beginning, the course and the end of their unity? "For whatever was written in former days was written for our instruction, that, by steadfastness and by the encouragement of the Scriptures we might have hope" (Rom. 15:4). This text of St. Paul undoubtedly alludes to everything that God caused to be recorded in the Bible, but what is particularly striking is that the verses which follow — their close connection with the preceding verse is shown by their taking up again the words "steadfastness and encouragement" — immediately focus attention on the question of Christian unity: "May the God of steadfastness and encouragement grant you to live in such harmony with one another, in accord with Christ Jesus, that together you may with one voice glorify the God and Father of our Lord Jesus Christ" (Rom. 15:5-6).

The testimony of the Bible is without doubt the most important reason for Christians to seek ways and means towards Christian peace and reconciliation. There are in fact many other reasons of a general religious, practical or even secular character which make themselves strongly felt today in the ecumenical movement, both within and outside the

Catholic Church. The idea of a united Christianity, working together in mutual harmony, finds ready support at a time when men are aspiring to ever greater unity in Europe and to world-wide co-operation in such spheres as science, culture, economics and politics. Men today are learning to see the world as a single entity, and it seems reasonable to them to regard Christianity too as a whole. There is also the important fact that Christianity is seriously threatened in the modern world by challenging ideologies and forces of violence, against which the only effective resistance would appear to be a firm union. These motives for Christian reunion cannot be dismissed out of hand, but they are secondary. They hold good for the present time, but they may well be transitory. Holy Scripture, on the other hand, shows us clearly why Christians must always, everywhere and in all circumstances be one. The Christians of the first generation may have found it easier to give themselves up to the ideal of one single Christian community for the whole **oikoumene,** that is, for the whole of the inhabited world, because of their experience of the secular Roman **oikoumene** in which they lived. But what really held them together was their "call in one hope," their devotion to the "one Lord, one faith, one baptism, one God and Father of us all" (Eph. 4:4-5). This decisive reason was proclaimed and affirmed for Christians of all generations by the Bible, with divine originality and authority.

Holy Scripture does not only provide the most pure inspiration for the search for an all-embracing unity. It also offers the authentic norms for the shaping of the course ahead. It finally provides the most secure guarantee for the success of the ecumenical movement and lays down a firm basis for our belief in the reunion which we are still not able to see. The reunion of all Christians who are baptized in Christ is a grace of God. The Bible not only teaches us intelligibly about this grace and its history; it also offers this teaching to us now in an instructive and encouraging way and provides us with the incentive to follow it. The Word of God in Holy Scripture brings about unity whenever it is heard in faith.

Scripture does not, however, achieve Christian unity at present. No Christian community can read the Bible in any other way than within its own tradition. The one Word of God is read, but the division between Christians remains. The writer of such a book as this, on Christian unity in the Bible, ought to select and contrast his texts so that all Christians might spontaneously recognize their "common salvation" (Jude 3) in them. But, as everyone knows, it is impossible to interpret the Bible in this way. Nonetheless, this book has been written with the aim of bringing closer the possibility of such a reading of Scripture.

The ideas which follow have been developed within the Catholic tradition, and they have been set down in this book above all so that Catholics may become more aware of the biblical testimony concerning Christian unity. My purpose has been to show what the Bible has to say both about the task of Catholics in preserving unity within their own Church and about their task in achieving reconciliation with all Christians.

These considerations are, however, also offered to Protestant Christians so that they may understand the views of us Catholics on Christian unity within the Bible more clearly. They may observe that Catholics also listen to their interpretation of Scripture and to their criticism. Listening to somebody implies taking him on trust. Sincerely placed trust in the Protestant method of and experience in scriptural exegesis does not, however, cancel out the typically Catholic interpretations that occur in this book, and for these I in turn ask for trust on the part of my Protestant readers, believing that they will treat them as genuine convictions in the matter of faith.

There are, however, reasons why we may hope not only that Catholics and Protestants will take each other on trust, but also that this mutual trust will bear results. Professor P. A. van Stempvoort, a Protestant, was able to write in the symposium, **Begegnung der Christen,** The present scientific situation permits us to assert with confidence; in the beginning was unity.

The nineteenth century view, based on the Hegelian interplay of thesis and antithesis, that it was not until the second century that a synthesis was achieved in the Church in the so-called early Catholicism, has been superceded by recent scientific research. The nineteenth century discovery of separate Petrine and Pauline communities in the New Testament, moving towards a later synthesis — a theory which was supported by "tendentious writings" such as the Acts of the Apostles — would be scientifically unacceptable today. It is quite clear to us now that the apostolic college of the Twelve and later apostolate of Paul formed a visible unity, even though it is possible to detect divisions here and there. The earlier apostolic group and the individual apostle who came later on the scene recognized each other in principle and found a way, by compromise, of working together. Many pasages in the New Testament provide visible evidence of the Church's growth as an ecumenical Christian empire within the Roman Empire. What the New Testament shows us is a visible unity."[1]

The biblical movement continues to grow within the Catholic Church. This and the cross-fertilization which results from the increasing cooperation between Catholic and Protestant biblical scholars are bound to act as an encouragement. Above all, we may see, in the present fact of God's calling us once again, through the Bible, to reunite, a benevolent sign that he will not refuse to give us what he is teaching us to ask for.

> "Thou wilt arise and have pity on Zion;
> It is the time to favor her; the appointed time
>   has come.
> For thy servants hold her stones dear;
> And have pity on her dust"   (Ps. 102:13-14).

1

THE BOOK OF UNITY

The Bible does not recognize the problem as to whether Christians ought together to form one real community. Nor does the Bible see any problem in the ability of so many Christians of different types, nationalities and cultures to form one genuine community. Holy Scripture speaks of Christian unity as a fact, the reality of which stems from the mystery of God's triune life, from the gift which God gave us in his unique Christ and from the task which will accompany Christians until the time of ultimate fulfillment.

In connection with the theme of Christian unity, the Bible does not simply communicate to us certain of God's decisive acts and words. On the contrary, it would be true to say that the Bible is wholly inspired by the idea of union. The main theme of the sacred books is that of reconciliation — the reconciliation between God and men and the reconciliation between men themselves. Reconciliation is the bringing together again of those who have become estranged from each other. The Authorized Version of the Bible translates the word "reconciliation" in Rom. 5:11 significantly by "atonement." The basis of this word is the concept "at one." The biblical theme of reconciliation, then, is a theme of "at-one-

ment," of making one. The Bible may rightly be
called the book of Christian unity, since the whole
aim of its testimony is, in the words of one of the
great biblical authors, "so that you may have fellowship with us, and our fellowship is with the Father
and with his son, Jesus Christ" (1 John 1:3).

There is, however, no single book or chapter in
the Bible to which the title "The Unity of the Christian Church" might be given. Nor is there any book
or chapter in which the nature and form of our
solidarity is systematically described as in the deed
of foundation of a company. Holy Scripture speaks
of Christian unity in the form of a history. This great
history embraces everyone and everything. It is the
history of God's "search" for communion with the
human race. It begins with the creation of man,
who was permitted to accompany God as his image
and likeness. It reaches its climax in the coming of
God the Son, who came to dwell among us as our
fellow-man. It ends with the gathering of all men
before the throne of God. The Bible bears witness
to God's aim of gathering all men around him in
this history of a divine initiative which gradually
reveals itself and is slowly developed and in which
mankind is actively involved in genuine partnership
with God.

The prelude to this history takes place in Para-
dise, where God created the first man, Adam, and
associated as intimately with him as with a son who
bore his image. God's intention in creating and
associating with Adam was to keep all men, in and

through Adam, in communion with himself and with each other. But Adam lost this communion with God and men became estranged from God and from each other. The confusion of tongues of Babel shows the division of a human race left to its own devices — "scattered abroad over the face of all the earth" (Gen. 11:9).

The history of the new and definitive unification of God with men begins with God's call to Abraham. God spoke to this man from Ur of the Chaldees, arousing faith in his heart and a sense of the reality of the communion with himself. Abraham became God's confidant (Gen. 18:17). He was called the "friend of God" (Judith 8:22). God took this first believer out of the chaos of nations and tribes in order to build up a new people for himself from him: "I will make of you a great nation" (Gen. 12:2). He gave him the name Abraham, meaning "father of a multitude of nations" (Gen. 17:5). God made a covenant of friendship with Abraham and his descendants, basing this on the faith of the "father of all who believe" (Rom. 4:11). The new community of God and mankind, and of men among themselves, slowly gained shape in the nation Israel. God renewed his covenant with the sons of the first man, with Isaac, Jacob, Moses and their descendants, and kept his people together by the expectation of the Messiah.

While he was fashioning his people, God kept them apart from other nations. This separation was not to be permanent, but God wished to prepare his people

in this way for the eventual coming of the Messiah,
when his community would be open to all who
wanted to join the Israel of God. He gradually revealed this ideal community which would commence
with the Messiah.

As a people, this new community was given God's
promise and his abiding presence, and as a people
it was also given the task of preserving this promise
and this divine presence and of passing them on.
As "his people" (Deut. 32:43; Ps. 94:14; Rom. 11:1, 2;
15:10), the community was an enclosed unity, a
family or a "house" in confrontation with the multiplicity of the pagan nations, the gentiles (Rom. 1:5;
15:11). This inner unity was expressed in the name
Israel, a personal name in the singular, first given
to Jacob as the ancestor of the people (Gen. 32:22-33;
Hos. 12:4 f.). Israel means the "first-born son of God"
(Exod. 4:22; Wis. 18:13) and implied that the people
was God's partner in the covenant and as such had
only one temple and one altar. In the age of the
kings, the prince personified the community and,
as the representative of the whole people, was given
the title of the "son of God" (2 Sam. 7:14; 1 Chron.
22:10; Ps. 2:7; 89:27). In several pasages, Yahweh
called Israel quite simply "his son" (Deut. 14:1; Isa.
1:2) or the "son of the living God" (Hos. 1:10).

> "It shall come to pass in the latter days
> That the mountain of the house of Yahweh
> Shall be established as the highest of the moun-
> tains,
> And shall be raised above the hills;

> And all the nations shall flow to it,
> And many peoples shall come, and say:
> Come, let us go up to the Mountain of Yahweh
> To the house of the God of Jacob;
> That he may teach us his ways,
> And that we may walk in his paths.
> For out of Zion shall go forth the law,
> And the word of Yahweh from Jerusalem.
> . . . They shall beat their swords into plough-
> shares,
> And their spears into pruning hooks;
> Nation shall not lift up sword against nation,
> Neither shall they learn war any more"
> (Isa. 2:2-4; cf. Mic. 4:1-3).

The climax and central point of this history of the making one of God and man is the Father's sending of his "beloved Son" (Matt. 17:5). In and through this act, God invited all men to come together around his "only Son" (1 John 4:9), to become themselves "children of God" (John 1:12-13) with the "first-born among many brethren" (Rom. 8:29). In Christ, the permanent meeting-place was made open and available to all, the one central point where Jacob's ladder led to the Father, "the house of God and the gate of heaven" (Gen. 28:17).

Not all Israelites responded to this new and decisive phase in the progressive realization of God's plan with mankind. A minority remained faithful to the Covenant and a small "Remnant" received Christ (Rom. 9:27; 11:4). This Remnant formed a little circle of believers, the new Israel under a "New Covenant" (Matt. 26:28). Micah prophesied this:

> "In that day, says Yahweh,
> I will assemble the lame
> And gather those who have been driven away,
> And those whom I have afflicted;
> And the lame I will make the Remnant,
> And those who were cast off a strong nation.
> And Yahweh will reign over them
> In Mount Zion, from this time forth and for
> evermore"
>
> (Mic. 4:6-7).

In this way, God accomplished his plan in and through Christ, "not for the nation (Israel) only, but to gather into one the children of God who are scattered abroad" (John 11:52), and thus to become "the Father of us all, who is above all and through all and in all" (Eph. 4:6).

At the beginning of this period of the fulfillment of God's plan, the apostle Paul declared that we were the object of his mercy, we "whom he has called, not from the Jews only, but also from the Gentiles. As indeed he says in Hosea, "Those who were not my people I will call 'my people,' and her who was not beloved I will call 'my beloved' . . . And in the very place where it was said to them, 'You are not my people,' they will be called 'sons of the living God'" (Rom. 9:24-26; cf. also Hos. 2:23; 1:10). The grace and the task that were given to Abraham's descendants were transferred to his spiritual heirs,

and once again as to a people.[2] Those who believe
in the saving event of Christ as proclaimed by the
apostles were "added" to the existing unity (Acts
2:41), just as the gentile proselites had previously
been incorporated into Israel.

The Bible, then, teaches us about Christian unity
by providing us with the history of a people, first
of the people of Israel and subsequently of the
"chosen race, the holy nation," drawn from all tribes
and races, "who once were no people, but now are
God's people" (1 Pet. 2:9-10). The saving message
of the Bible was therefore not in the first place revealed in the history of an individual soul, nor was it
primarily formulated in instructions to souls. On the
contrary, salvation was first and foremost proclaimed
and offered to, and fulfilled in a community. Individual human beings find communion with God in
and through their reception into the people of God.
The Bible also teaches us that, if we really are to
belong to the people of God, each of us must be
"circumcised" in our heart, that is, we must believe
in our heart, since the life of the community is
founded on faith in the God of reconciliation. At
the same time, the Bible also says that "not all who
are descended from Israel belong to Israel" (Rom.
9:6). In other words, a purely external membership
of the people of God, either that of the old or that
of the new Covenant, is in no way a guarantee of
true communion with God. At the same time, the
Bible also teaches us that we must be circumcised
in our flesh as well as in our hearts if we are to belong

to the people of the Covenant, in other words, that
faith must be accompanied by baptism, in which case
our reception will be ratified in a divine manner
by the gift of Christ's Spirit (Cf. Acts 2:38; 8:12,
36-38). Thus Holy Scripture leaves us in no doubt
whatever as to where the God of our salvation is to
be found. He dwells in the midst of his people, and
no one can come to him without belonging to the
community of his people. Thus God established
a house in the midst of this world, a house in which
he wished to gather all men, at one with him and
with each other:

> "And the foreigners who join themselves to
>   Yahweh
> To minister to him, to worship him
> And to love the Name of Yahweh,
> And to be his servants,
> Everyone who keeps the sabbath, and does
>   not profane it,
> And holds fast my Covenant —
> These I will bring to my holy mountain,
> And make them joyful in my house of prayer;
> Their burnt offerings and their sacrifices
> Will be accepted on my altar;
> For my house shall be called
> A house of prayer for all peoples.
> Thus says the Lord Yahweh,
> Who gathers the outcasts of Israel:
> I will gather yet others to him
> Besides those already gathered"   (Isa. 56:6-8).

The Bible deals with the subject of Christian

unity, then, in the form of a history, and this means
that human beings have their part to play in it.
Man's share in the history of salvation appears, at
least in part, to be that of an adversary rather than
that of a partner, insofar as he continually sets himself up in opposition to God's initiative and resists
God's attempts to fashion the human community.
"Jerusalem, Jerusalem, killing the prophets and ston-
ing those who are sent to you! How often would I
have gathered your children together as a hen gathers
her brood under her wings, and you would not!"
(Matt. 23:37; Luke 13:34). God's initiative, holding
out to all men unity with him and with each other,
is an offer to men who from birth are centered in
themselves and who can only very slowly be cured
of this self-centeredness. God established his community by overcoming a scattered humanity and by
conquering men who were divided in their hearts
against each other. Complete surrender in faith
and love is the active share required by God of his
partners in the building up of his community both in
ancient Israel and in the new Israel.

Whoever has received God's gift of sonship is
bound to experience this together with the other
sons of the same Father. Anyone who cuts himself
off from his brothers would seem not to have understood the gift he has received and thus not to have
received it properly: "He who loves is born of God
and knows God. He who does not love does not
know God, for God is love" (1 John 4:7-8).

Can God's initiative ever come to nothing when

it is left to men to come to God freely by joining his people? God's word never returns to him empty, but is always an everlasting sign (Cf. Isa. 55:11, 13). Since the time of Abraham, his offer has assumed a form in this world which will never be destroyed. What God has begun he will certainly fulfill. As Israel did not succumb under the threat of disunity, so also will the Church not succumb.

> "Of old thou didst lay the foundation of the earth,
> And the heavens are the work of thy hands.
> They will perish, but thou dost endure;
> They will all wear out like a garment.
> Thou changest them like raiment, and they pass away;
> But thou art the same, and thy years have no end.
> The children of thy servants shall dwell secure;
> And their posterity shall be established before thee"   (Ps. 102:25-28).

God's covenant with the community founded by him is everlasting: "I will not forget you. Behold, I have graven you on the palms of my hands; your walls are continually before me" (Isa. 49:15-16), and "the powers of death shall not prevail against it (my Church)" (Matt. 16:18), for "Lo, I am with you always, to the close of the age" (Matt. 28:20). God's power to bring men together is stronger than that of the "prince of this world," who has been overcome by Christ, to scatter and divide them. God's faithfulness to the covenant is our assurance of this, and the Holy Spirit, who descended upon the Church and whose presence in the Church is the "guarantee of our inheritance" (Eph. 1:14) is our safeguard of the "purpose of him who accomplishes all things according to the counsel of his will" (Eph. 1:11).

But, although this unity created by God among men will never succumb to the threat of complete disunity, it is nonetheless subject to human frailty — the recipients of this unity are weak men. The unity of the Church is holy and splendid. Coming from God, it is indestructible. But it is also very delicate, and the purer and more exalted it is, the more vulnerable it becomes. It is a gift which makes many demands of those who receive it. It must be accepted by believers in their inmost hearts, and it must at the same time be expressed outwardly in honest praise of God and in sincere communal confession of faith. It must manifest itself in effective brotherly love here and now. From the very beginning there have always been tensions both in ancient Israel and in the new Israel of God. From the beginning there have always been divisions and reunions. The unity of Christians is a gift of God, but it is a gift which must be brought to fulfillment by us. Is this not true of all God's gifts to mankind? God accomplishes his grace not only in us but also with us, and this is why the history of our salvation is sometimes full of light and at others full of shadow. Scripture describes both the light and the shadow, emphasizing that unity is a gift of God and warning us against everything that may impair this unity. In its accounts of events and its repeated warnings, the Bible condemns divisions and schisms and protests against factions, self-seeking, pride and all that can divide men against each other.

Thus the Bible gives us the history both of unity and of disunity, or rather of unity in spite of disunity, since it is the unity of God and man and of men among themselves which emerges in the end. In the end we shall all stand before God's throne and listen to the "great voice" saying: "Behold, the dwelling of God is with men, He will dwell with them, and they shall be his people, and God himself will be with them" (Rev. 21:3).

Now, however, we are still on the way. We are living in the time between the Ascension and the Lord's Second Coming. God knows how long our pilgrimage will last and how much time still remains to us "for the building up of the Body of Christ, until we all attain to the unity of the faith and of the knowledge of the Son of God, to mature manhood, to the measure of the stature of the fullness of Christ" (Eph. 4:12-13). The Church is still the people of God in a state of growth — "speaking the truth in love, we are to grow up in every way" (cf. Eph. 4:15), which means that the Church still has to grow in unity. The Church is still going through the often painful process both of preserving and of developing this unity and she still has the task of overcoming all that threatens her unity and of healing all the wounds that it sustains.

We have been given the Bible to nourish our faith
in Christian unity throughout this time of growth.
The Bible teaches us the profound reality of the
Christian community in such images and parables as
those of the one Shepherd and the one flock (John
10:16), the Vine and the branches (John 15:5) and
the one Body with many members (1 Cor. 12:12).
The Bible instructs us about the original mystery of
this unity in such passages as that containing Jesus'
prayer for us: "That they may all be one; even as thou,
Father, in me, and I in thee, that they also may be
in us" (John 17:21). The Bible shows us the shape of
this united Christianity in the early "Church of
Yahweh" which foreshadowed it (cf. for example,
Deut. 23:2, 3, 4), in the foundation of "my Church"
by Jesus (Matt. 16:18) and in the life of the early
Christian community which is described in the Acts
of the Apostles: "Devoting themselves to the apostles'
teaching and fellowship, to the breaking of bread
and the prayers" (Acts 2:42). The Bible holds this
unity up to us as a task which has to be accomplished,
constantly urging, encouraging and warning us to
have Christian love for each other: "With all lowliness and meekness, with patience, forbearing one
another in love" (Eph. 4:2), "Be of the same mind,
having the same love, being in full accord and of one
mind. Do nothing from selfishness or conceit, but in
humility, count others better than yourselves" (Phil.
2:2-3), to be "peaceable, gentle, open to reason, full
of mercy and good fruits, without uncertainty or
insincerity" (James 3:17), to attract him "who is weak
in faith" and not to engage in "disputes over opin-

ions" (Rom. 14:1). The Bible finally directs our attention to, and bids us hope firmly in "the holy city,
new Jerusalem, coming down out of heaven from
God, prepared as a bride adorned for her husband"
(Rev. 21:2).

How should the Catholic read this Book of unity?
Should he read it as one searching for unity? The
answer to this question will be partly negative and
at the same time partly strongly affirmative. The
Catholic Christian believes that the community of
those who "devote themselves to the apostles' teaching and fellowship, to the breaking of bread and
the prayers" (Acts 2:42) has always been realized
in the church that is still shepherded by the successors of the apostles who, in their turn, are gathered round the successor of St. Peter. This conviction
stems from the belief that is based on Christ's promise
that his community will, because of the power of the
Holy Spirit present in it, endure "for ever," until
the end of time (Cf. John 14:16).

This firm belief in the unity of the Church as a
present and actual reality which is realized in the
Church of Peter with its unbroken apostolic succes-
sion, has, however, to be fulfilled in the light of the
conscious understanding that it is a question not of
something which we ourselves have achieved, but of
an unceasing gift of God to us. We, for our part,
must never cease to show ourselves open and receptive to this gift. We must take the counsels which
Scripture gives us concerning Christian unity earnest-
ly to heart, and often in a spirit of penitence, and

we must pray during every celebration of the Eucharist: "Be thou pleased to keep and guide thy
Church in peace and unity" and "Deign to give her
peace and unity in accordance with thy will." It is
above all in this sense that we must be seekers of
unity — through prayer and brotherly love, we must
seek to build up the Church of Christ (Cf. 1 Cor.
14:12).

There is, however, another reason why Catholic
Christians should seek unity, a reason which, particularly at the present time, forces itself upon our
consciousness as believers with an almost irrestible
pressure. This is the fact of the continued existence
of so many groups of Christians outside the unity
of the Catholic Church, namely those which left the
ancient Church in the fifth, eleventh, and sixteenth
centuries. These Christians are, for those of us who
believe in the unity of the Catholic Church, a problem, a self-reproach and a task. Separated Christians
are also baptized into communion with Jesus Christ
(cf. Rom. 6:3) and "In one Spirit we were all baptized into one body and we have all been saturated
by the one Spirit" (1 Cor. 12:13). They are our
fellow-Christians and our brothers because of our
shared faith in Christ and baptism. The Second
Vatican Council has declared them to be "justified
by faith and incorporated into Christ in baptism;
they are therefore entitled to the name of Christians
and to be recognized by the sons and daughters of
the Catholic Church as brothers and sisters in the
Lord."[3] They have "the written word of God, the

life of grace, faith, hope and love, other interior
gifts of the Holy Spirit and also visible elements."
As far as their liturgical actions and their communities as such are concerned, the Council went on to
say that "the Spirit of Christ does not disdain to use
these as means of salvation." For this reason, we
have a genuine fellowship with them. This fellowship is, however, not the full, integral communion
which Christ offers to those who believe in him and
requires from them in return. We do not come
together with them around the one college of the
pastors of the Church and we do not say together
with them the one profession of faith. We cannot
therefore, share together in the "breaking of the
bread" which is the effective sign of partnership in
the one Body of Christ (1 Cor. 10:16-17). We are
thus certainly brothers, but at the same time in a
very real sense separated. The unity that was a
manifest fact at the time that the New Testament
was written has thus been impaired. As Catholics,
we believe on the one hand that the New Testament
unity has been perpetuated in the apostolic Church
of Peter. On the other hand, we are confronted
with the fact that this original unity has not been
preserved as an integral whole.

There can be no doubt whatever that this situation is completely contrary to the intention of the
Lord of the Church. It is a sinful situation which
is clearly opposed to God's testimony in the Book
of unity. We have to begin by questioning ourselves seriously and in a spirit of penitence about

our own share in the origins and the continuance of these separations, and Scripture will help and instruct us in this inquiry.

Then we have to consider the unity of the Church in which we believe in all its dimensions so that we may become aware of where and how we ceased to "attain to the unity of the faith and of the knowledge of the Son of God" (Eph. 4:13). Has the unity of the Catholic Church always been, and is it now in fact Catholic? Has it perhaps not become narrow, uniform, one-sided and inflexible? Was there really no place in this unity for the ancient traditions of the Christian East? Could the desires of the Reformers not be realized within the unity of the Church? The Second Vatican Council has openly admitted that the Catholic Church has failed "to express the fullness of Catholicism in every respect in the reality of life."[4] Thankful for the unity of the apostolic Church of Peter which has preserved the Spirit of Christ among us, we are faced now with the task of thinking about the meaning of this unity and the form which Christ desires it to take.

We cannot repair the divisions that came about in the eleventh and sixteenth centuries by returning to those periods and beginning again, nor can the churches and Christian communities which broke away from the apostolic community of Peter in the Catholic Church do this. Both the Catholic Church and the other churches have since then continued their history in successive generations of people and experiences, ideas, forms and expressions, and the

social climate has changed enormously. That is why
there can also be no question of a simple return on
the part of the other churches to the Catholic Church.
On the contrary, all the Christian communities must
grow towards a new form of the original New Testament unity. All must devote themselves anew to
a study of the "knowledge of the Son of God," and
as they grow in this knowledge, they will also in-
crease in the "unity of the faith." The Book of
Christian unity assures us of the faithfulness of the
Lord in this process and shows us the way to full
and universal unity, which it calls "peace." Our
hearkening to the Bible must not, however, result
in a quest to reduce everything to uniformity, but
should rather result in an urgent request for peace.
We should ask for peace as we pray in the liturgy
of the New Testament with the psalm of the Old:

> "Pray for the peace of Jerusalem!
> May they prosper who love you!
> Peace be within your walls,
> And security within your towers!
> For my brethren and companions' sake
> I will say, 'Peace be within you!'"
>
> (Ps. 122:6-8).

2

THE NEW COMMUNITY OF THE GOSPELS

As soon as Jesus appeared in public to begin to fulfill his messianic mission, he showed himself to the people of Israel accompanied by a group of disciples. These disciples were with him before he performed his first miracles, and before he set out on his journey to preach to the Israelites. They went with him always and in all the circumstances in which he found himself, from the time of his baptism in the Jordan to the time when, his task accomplished, he returned to the Father. This constant accompaniment of Jesus was one of the characteristic conditions of the apostolate, as the choice of a successor to Judas Iscariot clearly shows. Peter demanded that someone should be chosen from among "the men who have accompanied us during all the time that the Lord Jesus went in and out among us, beginning from the baptism of John until the day when he was taken up from us" (Acts 1:21-22). In fact, Jesus did not appear for a single moment alone as the Messiah. He was always surrounded by "his own," or "his disciples," from whom he soon chose the "Twelve." These men, whom Jesus called "my brethren" (Matt. 28:10), formed the core of the new community which

Jesus invited all men to join. Not everybody was called to belong to this special group within the community, but anyone desiring to follow Jesus was able to find him only among "his own." From the very beginning it was quite impossible for anyone to become his disciple in a strictly private sense.

Was it purely by accident or coincidence that Jesus appeared thus, or was it a manifestation of his own special mission? It is quite clear from the gospels that the latter was the case.

Jesus formed the inner circle of the apostles entirely on his own initiative. He summoned his candidates by calling upon them, briefly and authoritatively, to follow him. He himself bound them to his person and to each other. The formation of the group did not originate as the idea of a number of sympathizers desirous of joining a leader. There was also, as far as Jesus was concerned, no question of calling together a number of men who were spiritually in sympathy with each other. He first of all assembled these men, and only then began gradually to develop their mutual sympathy of mind and spirit around his own person. After an initial period of being, as it were, temporarily assembled, the group's permanent formation was undertaken: "He went up into the hills, and called to him those whom he desired; and they came to him. And he appointed twelve, to be with him, and to be sent out to preach" (Mark 3:13-14). Jesus was later able justly to claim: "You did not choose me, but I chose you" (John 15:16). From whatever point of view the subject is approached, it is clear that the group was formed by Jesus. He did not bring friends together, but transformed strangers into his and each others' friends. Towards the end of his period on earth, he assured them: "No longer do I call you servants (strangers), for the servant does not know what his master is doing; but I have called you friends, for all that I have heard from my Father I have made known to you" (John 15:15). The community, which Jesus left behind when he returned to the Father, and which went together and in one mind to the upper room, where "all with one accord devoted themselves to prayer" (Acts 1:12-14), was entirely his creation.

The inner circle which Jesus built up around his person was much more than an association of disciples. Indeed, it had all the characteristics of what we should now call "life in community."

Entry into this circle meant leaving one's own familiar environment. Peter and Andrew "immediately left their nets and followed him," James and John also "immediately left the boat and their father, and followed him" and Levi, who was sitting at the tax-house, "rose and followed him" (Matt. 4:17-22; Mark 1:16-20; 2:14; Luke 5:1-11; 5:27-28; John 1:35-51). All four evangelists testify to this fundamental change in the apostles' way of life, and what is more, they show that this happened at different occasions and list the circumstantial details: "house or brothers or sisters or father or mother or children or lands" (Matt. 19:29; Mark 10:29; Luke 18:29).

The disciples dissociated themselves completely from their own environment in order to join Jesus, and Peter had good reason to ask him, in the name of the Twelve, "Lo, we have left everything and followed you. What then shall we have?" (Matt. 19:27).

Joining Jesus' circle meant that the disciples were completely absorbed into Jesus' way of life and that they shared fully in everything that he undertook or experienced. They went with him on his missionary journeys, received private instructions from him and on one occasion preached themselves under his guidance. They shared in all his successes, but they also fled with him whenever opposition to his preaching took on a threatening form in Jerusalem or Judah. Their life with Jesus meant that their fate was really intimately bound up with his.

In their life of prayer too, the disciples were closely associated with Jesus. They went together to the temple or the synagogue. They were witnesses of his prayer, and were taught by him how and what to pray. They were the first to receive from him the new and distinctively Christian prayer, the "Our Father." Together with him they celebrated the annual feast of the Passover, the climax of the Israelites' religious experience.

Socially too, the group was one. The disciples shared in the hospitality which was offered to Jesus. They rested with him, took their meals with him and shared a common purse.

It may initially have seemed to them as if Jesus

was gathering them round him with the intention
of forming a school of disciples like those formed by
the teachers in Israel. But it soon became clear
that, unlike the teachers of these other schools,
whose disciples left when they had completed their
studies, Jesus aimed to keep his disciples permanently
together. He called his school the beginning of a
new kingdom, and his disciples were the first of a
new "community." The Twelve received a communal
mission, which they were also to carry out together.
The life in community was, it is true, not to last for-
ever in the form in which the disciples experienced
it in the years during which they were with Jesus.
The Lord was to return to the Father, and the disciples were to go out as his "witnesses in Jerusalem
and in all Judea and Samaria and to the end of the
earth" (Acts 1:8). Jesus commissioned them to bear
witness to him precisely as each others' brothers;
their testimony was not to be a series of private
declarations, but the "apostles' teaching" (Acts 2:42),
and each one of them was to speak about what they
had all witnessed (Cf. Acts 2:32). When, after several
years of working together in one place, they went
out separately, they did so in order to bring believers together — they did not, in other words, set
out with the aim of promulgating a view of life, but
with the aim of founding communities. The fact
that they were visibly one (cf. John 17:20-21) gave
the stamp of authenticity and truth to their testimony
and that of those who learned to believe in their
message: "A new commandment I give to you, that
you love one another; even as I have loved you, that

you also love one another. By this all men will
know that you are my disciples, if you have love for
one another" (John 18:34-35). This mutual brotherly
love was the proof and the condition of the disciples'
testimony of Jesus. The two things were indissolubly
linked to each other.

Jesus' community was something which was not
entirely unfamiliar to the disciples. They knew of
the existence of similar groups in the history of
Israel which had more or less withdrawn from the
community of the people as a whole. There were
the colonies of prophets at the time of Samuel (1
Sam. 10:10-12; 19:18-24) and, two centuries later, at
the time of the prophets Elijah and Elisha (2 Kings
2:3; 4:1), bands of men whose spiritual enthusiasm
had led to the formation of a special group and
whose way of life was quite different from that of
other Israelites, although their faith was the same.
What is more, there was, even at the time of Christ,
an extremely ascetic community living in Palestine,
in the neighborhood of the Dead Sea. The members
of this community, the Essenes, observed celibacy
and personal poverty, obeyed leaders whom they
themselves had chosen, refused to trade and to en-
list for military service, provided for their own upkeep by manual labor and devoted themselves entirely to a religious way of life according to the
Mosaic Law. Apart from the fact that this group
kept itself quite aloof from the ordinary people, it
was also different in other striking ways from Jesus'
community. In the first place, Jesus did not present

his way of life with his disciples as a more intense
or purer experience of the Law of Moses, but claimed
rather that it was the fulfillment of the promises
made in the Law, that it was the new and permanent
way of life — his community was the beginning of
the new kingdom. In the second place, the new
community was built up on Jesus' person. He spoke
of "following me," of "leaving everything for my
sake," of "leaving everything in my name." The
community would endure as long as the disciples
remained in him and he in them. The disciples would
remain together insofar as they were "in him." Their
prayer would be heard and answered by the Father
if they asked him in Jesus' name. He would be
among them "when two or three were gathered
together in his name." In his name, too, they were
to preach, baptize and perform miracles. This bond,
uniting them to the person of Jesus, was the power
and the authority of their preaching: "He who hears
you hears me, and he who rejects you rejects me"
(Luke 10:16). Those who opposed the new kingdom
of God would only have to strike the Shepherd, and
the flock would be scattered. (Cf. Matt. 26:31).

Jesus gradually made his disciples aware that the
messianic reconciliation between God and men would
come about in and through a community, a new
community which had as its origin and its constant
central point the incarnate Son of the Father. All
men were invited to join this community. The
Twelve came to realize that they were called to form
the first generation, the foundation members of this
community.

Jesus taught them this in a practical and direct way: "You are not to be called rabbi, for you have one teacher, and you are all brethren. And call no man your father on earth, for you have one Father, who is in heaven" (Matt. 23:8-9). This statement of the Lord characterizes the experience of Christian togetherness by comparing it with a primary form of human association, that of brotherhood based on blood-relationship.

In the first instance, Jesus was making use here of an Old Testament idea. It was their feeling of clan relationship that led in the first place to the Israelites regarding each other as brothers. This was of course also the case with other nations, but in Israel this feeling was reinforced by the religious conviction that she had been chosen as a nation by Yahweh and brought together by him. The brotherhood of Israel, then, was based above all on the grace of having a common Father in Yahweh: "Have we not all one father? Has not the one God created us? Why then are we faithless to one another?" (Mal. 2:10). Because of this vision, Israel meant the "son of God," the "first-born" and "his son" (Cf. p. 10). The people realized that "Yahweh your God bore you, as a man bears his son, in all the way" (Deut. 1:31) and that "as a man disciplines his son, Yahweh your God disciplines you" (Deut. 8:5; Prov. 3:12). God addressed Israel as a father speaks to his son: "I thought you would call me, My Father, and would not turn from following me" (Jer. 3:19).

Israel knew that her God was the Creator of

all men and thus the Father of all men, but she was at the same time aware of the existence of a special bond with this universal Father based on Abraham's election and the Covenant, which made for a more intimate brotherhood among the Israelites who believed in Yahweh.

The New Covenant is an extension of the Old, and Jesus simply took over the linguistic usage of the Old Covenant and its meaning — "brother" meant one's Jewish or Christian fellow-believer. Sometimes he used the word in a stricter sense for his disciples, that is, in the sense in which it was currently used in the rabbinical schools (Cf. Luke 22:31; Matt. 28:10). He also gave a new meaning to the idea of brotherhood when he used the word not to indicate a blood-relationship but to, point to the fulfillment of the will of the Father: "Whoever does the will of God is my brother, and sister, and mother" (Mark 3:31-35). This state of listening to and keeping God's word (cf. Luke 11:28) was for Jesus the most intimate relationship of all.

The young Christian community understood the meaning which Christ gave to the word brother: "For all who are led by the Spirit of God are sons of God . . . You have received the spirit of sonship. When we cry, 'Abba! Father!' it is the Spirit himself bearing witness with our spirit that we are children of God, and if children, then heirs, heirs of God and fellow heirs with Christ" (Rom. 8:14-17). If brotherhood within Israel was the result of God's special

fatherhood in respect of the people of his choice, the
idea of divine fatherhood gained a new dimension
in the Christian community. The fatherhood of God
the Father, "from whom every family in heaven
and on earth is named" (Eph. 3:15) was revealed
to us as having been realized originally in the Son,
the "beloved" (Matt. 17:5) and the "only" Son (John
1:14, 18). To whom else did God ever say: "You are
my son, today I have begotten you" (Ps. 2:7) and "I
will be his father, and he shall be my son" (2 Sam.
7:14)? (Cf. also Heb. 1:5). It is, however, only in and
through Christ that God's fatherhood is real for us.
The Spirit — of the Son (Gal. 4:6), of Christ (Rom.
8:9), of the Lord (2 Cor. 3:17) and of sonship (Rom.
8:15) — is poured into our hearts and causes us to
cry "Abba! Father!" because of the "mind" that we
have "in Christ Jesus" (Phil. 2:5; 1 Cor. 2:16). The
very real sense in which Christ was appointed as
the "first-born among many brethren" (Rom. 8:29)
by his Father is thus apparent. Thus, "he who sancti-
fies (Christ) and those (we) who are sanctified have
all one origin (the Father). That is why he (Christ)
is not ashamed to call them (us) brethren, saying, 'I
will proclaim thy name to my brethren, in the midst
of the congregation I will praise thee'" (Heb. 2:11-12;
Cf. also Ps. 22:22). Christ "had to be made like his
brethren in every respect" to realize this grace in
us (Heb. 2:17).

Our grace is the gift of "that one man Jesus Christ"
and we receive it in abundance "through the one
man Jesus Christ" (Rom. 5:15, 17). Thus, from the

one new man, the new and definitive brotherhood of men grew.[6]

The basic plan, according to which messianic salvation was to be accomplished, began gradually to emerge — God's universal fatherhood was to come to all men through the incarnate Son, who was able to unite all men as brothers to himself, and for his sake also to each other. The lines forming this plan were closely interwoven with each other — to reject Christ meant to shut oneself off from the Father, and to refuse to forgive one's brother meant to receive no forgiveness from the Father (Cf. John 15:23; Matt. 6:15). Jesus taught his disciples about God's fatherhood in a completely new way, as only he, God's "only Son," was able to teach them. At the same time, however, he taught them to pray in the plural, to "our" Father, for the gift of "our daily bread," for forgiveness of "our trespasses, as we forgive them that trespass against us" and for "our" exemption from temptation and from the evil threatening "us" (Cf. Matt. 6:9-13).

The gospels, in which salvation is revealed and offered to us, have an entirely concrete form which cannot be misunderstood. They show us Jesus as the only one by whom we can be saved, but they never show us Jesus alone — the Jesus of the gospels is always with "his own." This is not a secondary or accidental aspect of Revelation — it is an essential aspect. Jesus is the mediator of God's fatherhood to men precisely by making them his brothers and thus each others' brothers. No man can come to the

Father unless he comes through the Son, and no man can approach the Son without joining his brotherhood. According to the gospels, it is impossible to be a Christian purely as an individual. The precise function of the inner group of the apostles will be discussed in greater detail at a later stage; the principal aim of the present chapter is to draw attention to the striking fact that the historical gospels are presented in the concrete form of a human togetherness. Even those who were not members of the inner group of the twelve apostles, but who belonged to the wider circle of Jesus' disciples, shared in salvation because of their relationships with him, with the Twelve and with each other. These relationships were not based merely on spiritual affinity; they were relationships which made themselves felt in the daily practice of Christian life. "If you are offering your gift at the altar, and there remember that your brother has something against you, leave your gift there before the altar and go; first be reconciled to your brother, and then come and offer your gift" (Matt. 5:23-24).

This, then, is the first impression that we have if we look through the gospels searching for the form of God's work of reconciliation — that God reveals himself in Jesus with "his own." The gospels also give us a deeper insight into this revelation in the accounts they provide of Jesus' parables and tasks, and by their descriptions of the external form which Jesus gave to his community. The most striking portrayal in the gospels of this work of reconciliation is, however, the story of Jesus' perfect giving away of himself in the sacrifice of his life, which he offered on the one hand out of love for the Father (cf. John 10:17-18; 14:30-31), and on the other out of love for his friends (Cf. John 15:13-14).

3

ONE SHEPHERD AND ONE FLOCK

Among the most graphic of our Lord's pronouncements about his solidarity with "his own" and about his followers' mutual solidarity are those provided by the parables of the shepherd and his flock.

The words "flock," "sheep" and "herd" have unfortunate associations nowadays. We speak disparagingly of the "herd mentality" and of people behaving "like a flock of sheep." The words have acquired a negative meaning, indicating an absence of personal initiative and a defective sense of individual responsibility. In the Bible, however, the word "flock" has none of these associations. In biblical times, everyone was familiar with the idea of the flock as part of his daily experience, and the image of the flock immediately called to mind the idea of an intimately shared destiny, a fate shared both by the shepherd and his sheep and by the sheep among themselves.

The flock is the type of the peaceful society of many equals who manage to support and feed themselves and continue to exist precisely because they keep together. The existence of the flock without its shepherd is inconceivable. It was he who kept the flock together, who went out every day ahead of the flock to enable it to find food, who protected it from all threat of danger, who watched over it at night-time and who was constantly busy throughout the whole day "gathering" it. This "gathering" of the flock was quite literally a matter of vital importance for sheep, since a sheep which became separated from the flock was certainly doomed to die. In the same way, the existence of a shepherd without his flock is also inconceivable. He lived not only with his flock, but also for it, and his livelihood depended on it. He was one with his sheep.

For the Israelites, the image of the shepherd and his flock had very strong religious associations. The image of Yahweh as the "Shepherd of Israel" called to mind the single idea of the intimate and indissoluble bond between God and his people and the solidarity of the people itself (Cf. Gen. 48:15-16; 49:24; Hos. 4:16; Mic. 7:14). The image goes back originally to the very birth of the people of Israel as a nation, when Yahweh brought the twelve tribes out of Egypt, gathered them into one flock during the long period of separation in the desert, and finally went ahead of them, in the daytime as a cloud and by night as a pillar of light, and led them to the rich pasture of the promised land (Cf. Exod. 13:21-22; Ps. 78:52-54). When the people returned from the Babylonian captivity, the prophets again saw Yahweh as a shepherd gathering his scattered sheep together and placing them under his protection in order to lead them to their country: "I will

surely gather all of you, O Jacob, I will gather
the remnant of Israel; I will set them together like
sheep in a fold, like a flock in its pasture, a noisy
multitude of men. He who opens the breach will
go up before them; they will break through and
pass the gate, going out by it. Their king will pass
on before them, Yahweh at their head" (Mic. 2:12-13;
cf. also Isa. 40:10-11).

The image of the shepherd and his flock gave the
believing Israelite a number of assurances concerning
his faith. Just as a flock was established on the
initiative of a shepherd, and thus became his property, so Israel was bound to "know that Yahweh
is God! It is he that made us, and we are his; we
are his people, and the sheep of his pasture" (Ps.
100:3), and to "kneel before Yahweh, our Maker!
For he is our God, and we are the people of his
pasture, and the sheep of his hand" (Ps. 95:6-7). Just
as a shepherd cares for his flock, gives it pasture
and keeps it on the right path, so Israel confessed:
"Yahweh is my shepherd, I shall not want; he makes
me to lie down in green pastures. He leads me be-
side still waters; he restores my soul. He leads me in
paths of righteousness for his name's sake. Even
though I walk through the valley of the shadow of
death, I fear no evil; for thou art with me; thy rod
and thy staff, they comfort me" (Ps. 23:1-4). Again,
as a shepherd keeps watch at night-time over the
sheep-fold, the psalmist was able to assure Israel:
"Behold, he who keeps Israel will neither slumber
nor sleep" (Ps. 121:4). Finally, like a shepherd who

is intent on keeping his flock together and who constantly goes out to gather the sheep that have become scattered back into the fold, Yahweh was able to say to his people, at a time when they had become dispersed: "Behold, I, I myself will search for my sheep, and will seek them out. As a shepherd seeks out his flock when some of his sheep have been scattered abroad, so will I seek out my sheep; and I will rescue them from all places where they have been scattered on a day of clouds and thick darkness. And I will bring them out from the peoples, and gather them from the countries, and will bring them into their own land; and I will feed them on the mountains of Israel" (Ezek. 34:11-13). Jeremiah, too, was able to say of Yahweh: "He who scattered Israel will gather him, and will keep him as a shepherd keeps his flock" (Jer. 31:10).

Yahweh carried out this pastoral function by means of his prophets, kings and priests. When Moses realized that the end of his life was approaching, he asked Yahweh to appoint a successor, "who shall go out before them and come in before them, who shall lead them out and bring them in; that the congregation of Yahweh may not be as sheep which have no shepherd" (Num. 27:17). Later on, Yahweh gave David the task of carrying out this pastoral function: "He chose David his servant, and took him from the sheepfolds; from tending the ewes that had young he brought him to be the shepherd of Jacob his people, of Israel his inheritance" (Ps. 78:70-71).

King David was the prototype of the Messiah who was to be sent by Yahweh to be the true shepherd of the people. The monarchy had, of its very nature, a strongly pastoral aspect for nomadic people who lived with their flocks and gained their livelihood from them. At the same time, the image of the figure with a shepherd's staff walking at the head of his flock had a certain royal quality. When the promises had been fulfilled, "I will set up over them one shepherd, my servant David, and he shall feed them and be their shepherd" (Ezek. 34:23). David had already been dead and buried for four centuries when Ezekiel made this prophecy in God's name, so that it is clear that he is alluding, in his use of the name of David, to David's descendant, the Messiah. Jeremiah also spoke of the same prospect of the one shepherd caring for the flock: "I will gather the remnant of my flock out of all the countries where I have driven them, and I will bring them back to their fold . . . Behold, the days are coming, says Yahweh, when I will raise up for David a righteous Branch, and he shall reign as king and deal wisely, and shall execute justice and righteousness in the land" (Jer. 23:3-5). When the time of the fulfillment of the promises had dawned, the Messiah was also announced to Mary as the Son of David who was to "reign over the house of Jacob for ever" (Luke 1:33).

The prophet Ezekiel was also to say, about the unity which Yahweh was to bring about in the messianic time: "Behold, I will take the people of

Israel from the nations among which they have gone, and will gather them from all sides, and bring them to their own land; and I will make them one nation in the land, upon the mountains of Israel; and one king shall be king over them all; and they shall be no longer two nations, and no longer divided into two kingdoms . . . My servant David shall be king over them; and they shall all have one shepherd" (Ezek. 37:21-22, 24; cf. also Hos. 1:11).

In revealing himself as a shepherd and in calling his disciples his flock, Jesus not only evoked an extremely concrete and intelligible image in the minds of those who heard him, he also appealed strongly to their religious experience in Israel's history and to their messianic expectations. All the characteristic features of the Old Testament image were present in Jesus' use of it, but especially the unique bond between the shepherd and his flock and the solidarity of the sheep gathered round the one shepherd.

It is remarkable how frequently Jesus made himself known as a shepherd in the gospels. Whenever he revealed his feelings about his disciples or about those whom he would have liked to see among the band gathered round him, he tended to express himself in the terminology of the shepherd. To encourage his disciples at a time when they were feeling uncertain, he said, for example: "Fear not, little flock, for it is your Father's good pleasure to give you the kingdom" (Luke 12:32). He looked on "the lost sheep of the house of Israel" (Matt. 10:6; 15:24) with the eye and the heart of a shepherd, and he had pity on the crowds who were "like sheep without a shepherd" (Mark 6:34; Matt. 9:36). To express his anxious care for a disciple who was going astray, he used the parable of the shepherd who had lost one of his hundred sheep: "Does he not leave the ninety-nine on the hills and go in search of the one that went astray? And if he finds it, truly, I say to you, he rejoices over it more than over the ninety-nine that never went astray" (Matt. 18:12-13; Luke 15:4-7). He saw himself too as a shepherd at the Last Judgment, separating the sheep from the goats (Matt. 25:31-46). Before his return to the Father, he entrusted his own to Peter with the words: "Feed my lambs, tend my sheep" (John 21:15-17). The disciples understood this manner of speaking so well that they spontaneously referred to their later apostolic work in terms of flock, feeding and sheep (Cf., for example, Acts 20:28; Eph. 4:11; 1 Pet. 2:25; 5:2-4; Heb. 13:20; Apoc. 12:5).

Jesus himself provides a very full exposition of the image of the shepherd and his flock in the tenth chapter of St. John's gospel. The emphatic opening "Truly, truly," followed by "I say to you" indicates that this is an important statement. The exposition is constructed of three parables. The language of the image is subject to certain variations, but the parables are clearly complementary to each other.

"Truly, truly, I say to you, he who does not enter the sheepfold by the door but climbs in by another way, that man is a thief and a robber; but he who enters by the door is the shepherd of the sheep. To him the gatekeeper opens; the sheep hear his voice, and he calls his own sheep by name and leads them out. When he has brought out all his own, he goes before them, and the sheep follow him, for they know his voice. A stranger they will not follow, but they will flee from him, for they do not know the voice of strangers" (John 10:1-5).

Jesus thus reveals himself as the one shepherd, the guide and leader of men sent by the Father. This is the principal theme of this and of the two parables which follow. In the first parable, Jesus makes use of a comparison derived from what actually happened in the morning in the sheepfold. The fold generally consisted of an uncovered space, surrounded by the rear walls of various buildings or by a low wall. There was a single opening which served both as the entrance to and as the way out of the fold. A large sheepfold was used by several shepherds for their flocks. One of their number, or a servant, mounted guard at the door. A legitimate shepherd would come to the fold in the morning and go in by the door. He would give his own call and, hearing it, the sheep of his own flock would come to him. Others, who wanted to appropriate sheep fraudulently, did not enter by the door of the fold, and had no need to use their voices, since the sheep would not recognize the call and would not follow.

Jesus, however, approached "the sheep of the house of Israel" in an open and honest way. He did not force himself upon them and appropriated noth-

ing, but began to speak to them in the name of the
Father and made it clear that "if this man were not
from God, he could do nothing" (John 9:33). Later,
he was able to testify before the high priest: "I have
spoken openly to the world; I have always taught in
the synagogues and in the temple, where all Jews
come together; I have said nothing secretly" (John
18:20). All those who really believed recognized his
voice, and his words echoed in the pure hearts of
those who were familiar with the words of Yahweh.
Peter expressed this conviction at the conclusion of
Christ's sermon on the Eucharist, which had given
offense to many: "You have the words of eternal
life; and we have believed and have come to know,
that you are the Holy One of God" (John 6:68-69).
Recognizing God's voice, those who believed recalled the messianic promise: "I will save my flock,
they shall no longer be a prey; and I will judge
between sheep and sheep. And I will set up over
them one shepherd, my servant David, and he shall
feed them and be their shepherd" (Ezek. 34:22-23).
Thus those who truly believe come of their own
accord to Jesus, and the reason for this is because
they know his voice. The recognition of Jesus'
voice — being called by him and hearing this call
— is the reason for the existence of the fellowship
between Jesus and "his own" and the mutual fellowship of the disciples themselves. On the eve of his
departure from the world, the Lord was to say to
the Father: "I have manifested thy name to the
men whom thou gavest me out of the world; thine
they were, and thou gavest them to me, and they

have kept thy word. Now they know that everything that thou hast given me is from thee; for I have given them the words which thou gavest me, and they have received them and know in truth that I came from thee; and they have believed that thou didst send me" (John 17:6-8; cf. also John 6:44-46; Isa. 54:13; Jer. 31:33-34). Faith is the beginning of all salvation. Faith in Jesus as the Shepherd sent by God brought many together around him. One of the most ancient titles of the Church is also "the assembly of the faithful."

An elucidation of the first parable follows in the second. "Truly, truly, I say to you, I am the door of the sheep. All who came before me are thieves and robbers; but the sheep did not heed them. I am the door; if any one enters by me, he will be saved, and will go in and out and find pasture. The thief comes only to steal and kill and destroy; I came that they may have life, and have it abundantly" (John 10:6-10).

Here Jesus calls himself the door of the sheepfold. When the sheep were going in and out of the fold, the shepherd would stand in the opening in the surrounding wall, and each sheep would have to pass by him. In this way a shepherd could keep his own sheep together and see to it that they all went together to pasture in the morning and were all safely back in the fold at night. In calling himself the door, Jesus did not essentially change the image of himself as the shepherd, since the shepherd was the living door of the sheepfold. By focusing attention

on this special function of the shepherd, Jesus revealed himself as the "Leader and Savior" (Acts 5:31)
and as the "Author of life" (Acts 3:15), in other
words, as the one who gives and guarantees life. The
Greek word for "leader" really means the founder
and prototypal hero from whom everything proceeds.
At the same time, Jesus revealed himself as the one
entrance to "abundant life," and later he was to say:
"I am the way, and the truth, and the life; no one
comes to the Father, but by me" (John 14:6).

What Jesus was saying, then, in this continuation
of the first parable, was that the community of faith,
which keeps many men together like a flock and
binds them to him and to each other, is a fellowship
of life in God.

At the same time, he contrasted himself with
others who wished to gain control of the "sheep of
Israel." In the first parable, he referred to the "thief
and robber" who was a "stranger" to the sheep. His
resumption of this criticism in the second parable
must have made his listeners think immediately of
the verdict which Yahweh had already pronounced
again and again on the bad leaders of Israel and
at the same time it must have reminded them of the
messianic promises concerning the "true Shepherd."
To prepare Israel for the coming of the "one shepherd, my servant David," who was to feed them
(Ezek. 34:23), Yahweh had appointed leaders "to be
the shepherd of his people" (Ps. 78:71). But Yahweh
had been obliged to intervene repeatedly throughout
Israel's history, since these leaders again and again

had made use of the pastoral function entrusted to them in their own interests, with the result that the Israelites had in fact become scattered "like sheep . . . afflicted for want of a shepherd" (Zech. 9:16; 10:2). Israel's leaders had sold the people like shepherds who had no pity on their sheep, saying "Blessed be Yahweh, I have become rich." Prefiguring the Messiah, the prophet Zechariah had been appointed as the shepherd of Israel and had received two staffs from Yahweh, one named "Goodness" and the other "Union." The negligent shepherds, however, refused to accept Zechariah and gave him thirty silver shekels in order to be rid of him. But the sheep were also recalcitrant, and Zechariah broke both his staffs and concluded: "Strike the shepherd, that the sheep may be scattered" (Cf. Zech. 11:3-17; 13:7).

In the post-exilic period too, Yahweh reproached Israel: "The dogs have a mighty appetite; they never have enough. The shepherds also have no understanding; they have all turned to their own way, each to his own gain, one and all" (Isa. 56:11).

Yahweh also censured the leaders of the people through the prophet Jeremiah and at the same time pointed to the definitive shepherd, the Messiah: "Woe to the shepherds who destroy and scatter the sheep of my pasture! . . . I will gather the remnant of my flock . . . Behold, the days are coming when I will raise up for David a righteous Branch, and he shall reign as king and deal wisely, and shall execute justice and righteousness in the land" (Jer. 23:1-5).

The fiercest of all Yahweh's protests were voiced by Ezekiel. The negligence of Israel's leaders had resulted in the flock becoming alienated from their God and worshiping idols. The unity of the flock had been destroyed and it had become scattered. Yahweh was to restore his people's religion and the unity of the flock by sending the Messiah: "I will cleanse them; and they shall be my people, and I will be their God"; the Messiah was to gather them together again like a shepherd: "They shall all have one shepherd" (Ezek. 37:21-24).

Another passage in the same prophetic book shows clearly what Jesus intended to do with the "thieves and robbers" and how he would associate with his sheep. This passage also contains an echo of the later dismissal of the priests and pharisees which would occur when the authentic and permanent shepherd had come. Jesus himself referred to all these prophecies when he revealed himself to his listeners. "Thus says Yahweh the Lord: Ho, shepherds of Israel, who have been feeding yourselves! Should not shepherds feed the sheep? You eat the fat, you clothe yourselves with the wool, you slaughter the fatlings; but you do not feed the sheep. The weak you have not strengthened, the sick you have not healed, the crippled you have not bound up, the strayed you have not brought back, the lost you have not sought, and with force and harshness you have ruled them. So they were scattered, because there was no shepherd; and they became food for all the wild beasts: My sheep were scattered, they wandered over all the mountains and on every high hill; my sheep were scattered over all the face of the earth, with none to search or seek for them. Therefore, you shepherds, hear the word of Yahweh: As I live, says Yahweh the Lord, because my sheep have become a prey, and my sheep have become food for all the wild beasts, since there was no shepherd; and because my shepherds have not searched for my sheep, but the shepherds have fed themselves, and have not fed my sheep; therefore, you shepherds, hear the word of Yahweh: Thus says Yahweh the Lord, Behold, I am against the shepherds; and I will require my sheep at their hand, and put a stop to their feeding the sheep; no longer shall the shepherds feed themselves. I will rescue my sheep from their mouths, that they may not be food for them. For thus says Yahweh the Lord: Behold, I, I myself will search for my sheep, and will seek them out. As a shepherd seeks out his flock when some of his sheep have been scattered abroad, so will I seek out my sheep; and I will rescue them from all places where they have been scattered on a day of clouds and thick darkness. And I will bring them out from the peoples, and gather them from the countries, and will bring them into their own land . . . I myself will be the shepherd of my sheep, and I will make them lie down, says Yahweh the Lord. I will seek the lost, and I will bring back the strayed, and I will bind up the crippled, and I will strengthen the weak, and the fat and strong I will watch over; I will feed them in justice" (Ezek. 34:2-16).

This prophecy concludes with the promise of the Messiah, who was to be an "authentic shepherd" for them. These words are echoed in the last of the three interconnected parables under discussion.

"I am the good shepherd. The good shepherd lays down his life for his sheep. He who is a hireling and not a shepherd, whose own the sheep are not, sees the wolf coming and leaves the sheep and flees; and the wolf snatches them and scatters them. He flees because he is a hireling and cares nothing for the sheep. I am the good shepherd; I know my own and my own know me, as the Father knows me and I know the Father; and I lay down my life for the sheep. And I have other sheep, that are not of this fold; and I must bring them also, and they will heed my voice. So there shall be one flock, one shepherd" (John 10:11-16).

The Greek word, translated in English by "good," is the same as the word meaning "authentic" used by Ezekiel. In the context of "good shepherd," "good" should not be thought of as meaning "gentle" or "kind," but as meaning "real" or "authentic." This meaning is also clear from the contrast with the hireling, who was not rejected because he was not kind and good-hearted, but because he was not a true, authentic shepherd.

Jesus' reference to his own imminent death also shows that he himself was the authentic shepherd. Those who heard the parable were shortly to witness his laying down of his life for them, and it

would be clear from this event that he was the real
and unique shepherd. Jesus' death on the Cross for
his flock would also be the fulfillment of those
prophecies which foretold the attempts on the part
of the leaders of the people to banish the shepherd
sent by God from his flock by paying him off with
thirty pieces of silver and the "striking of the shepherd and the scattering of the sheep" (Cf. Zeph.
11:3-17; 13:7). Jesus' dying to give life to his sheep
was to be the climax of his pastoral activity.

When the leaders of Israel wanted to be rid of
Jesus, the high priest, Caiaphas, unwittingly uttered
a prophecy in which he alluded to Jesus as the
shepherd who, by dying, was to gather the sheep
and thus save them: "So the chief priests and the
Pharisees gathered the council, and said, 'What are
we to do? For this man performs many signs. If
we let him go on thus, every one will believe in
him . . .' But one of them, Caiaphas, who was high
priest that year, said to them, 'You know nothing
at all; you do not understand that it is expedient for
you that one man should die for the people, and
that the whole nation should not perish.' He did
not say this of his own accord, but being high priest
that year he prophesied that Jesus should die for
the nation, and not for the nation only, but to gather
into one the children of God who are scattered
abroad" (John 11:47-52). Thus Jesus became the
"pioneer of men's salvation perfected through suffering" (Heb. 2:10) and the "great shepherd of the
sheep, by the blood of the eternal covenant" (Heb.
13:20).

In the third of these three parables, then, Jesus throws fresh light on the bond existing between him and his own. In the first parable, he defined this as a recognition of his voice whenever he called. In this last parable, he says that the recognition is on both sides. It is not simply a question of knowing "who is who," but rather a question of mutual understanding based on affection and sympathy. It is not merely, and certainly not even first and foremost, a question of understanding the words spoken, but of a mutual interpenetration of persons speaking. Faith, which is the basis of all unity, does not consist of knowing concepts, but above all of understanding Christ. A knowledge of facts and articles of faith are, of course, implied in this, but they are his facts, and articles of faith in him.

There is, of course, a great difference between the knowledge that Jesus has of us and the knowledge that we, as believers, have of him. The Shepherd "knows" his sheep before they know him — we "recognize" that he has known us. Thus, St. Paul could write: "But now that you have come to know God, or rather to be known by God" (Gal. 4:9), and "But if one loves God, one is known by him" (1 Cor. 8:3). The agreement to which Jesus alludes here is that it is a mutual knowing between persons, a knowing based on mutual affection and dedication, arising from an inner relationship. In the first of the parables, Jesus says that the shepherd "calls his own sheep by name." This is a clear indication of the personal nature of the relationship between the shepherd and the flock. Although this knowledge bears some resemblance to that by which partners in marriage know each other and parents know their children, it is at the same time a contact between the Lord and his own at the supramundane level. Jesus speaks of this knowledge as an extension of the mutual knowledge existing between the Father and the Son. He is thus drawing our attention to a mystery, namely to the mystery of our life in God which is beyond our comprehension. In the sublime unity of the one God three different persons reveal themselves fully to each other in a way which surpasses our understanding, and are perfectly united to each other without being lost in each other. Jesus points to the mystery of God in order to make us aware of the gift of grace and the mystery of his unity with those who believe in him.

This reference to the mystery of the unity of God at the same time teaches us about the origin of the unity which Jesus wishes to realize on earth. This unity is a gift of God. "My sheep hear my voice, and I know them, and they follow me; and I give them eternal life, and they shall never perish, and no one shall snatch them out of my hand. What my Father has given to me is the greatest of all, and no one is able to snatch it out of the Father's hand. I and the Father are one" (John 10:27-30). The unity of the faithful gathered around Jesus comes from God, and that is why it is indestructible. Jesus was to reveal even more about this in his parting words to his own at the Last Supper.

All are called to share in this unity of the one Shepherd with the one flock. It was a direct continuation of the unity existing between the sheep of Israel and their Shepherd, although it was not manifested in every respect in precisely the same way, since Jesus had "other sheep, that are not of this fold," and these too he had to feed. This unity is a gift of God and it is accomplished in us through faith in the Shepherd whom God has sent and through our joining his flock.

4

MY COMMUNITY

What Jesus himself has to say about the Shepherd
and his flock directs our attention particularly to
the interior aspect of the fellowship with him and
gathered around him. It was assumed that this
fellowship would appear as such in a visible form,
since there was no question of the formation of a
group of purely spiritual beings, but of a group of
men. The external form in which this fellowship was
manifested was, moreover, suggested by the very
image of the shepherd with his flock, an image
which called to mind a state of togetherness em-
bracing the whole of life, and which had indeed
already acquired a visible form in the people of
Israel. But, in the case of the fellowship with Jesus,
the emphasis was above all on the spiritual aspect.
Jesus' own words drew attention in the first place
to the form of this spiritual fellowship. Yet the external form did not exist alongside this interior fellowship. On the contrary, the inner solidarity between Jesus and his flock was experienced in the
outward form. It was in the outward form of the
community too that this inner solidarity was realized
in the world and proclaimed to mankind in the world.
This close connection between the interior aspect

and the exterior form of the Christian community
was stressed by the Lord himself when he required
Peter to make an explicit confession of faith before
proclaiming the establishment of his Church.

"Now when Jesus came into the district of Caesarea
Philippi, he asked his disciples, 'Who do men say
that the Son of man is?' And they said, 'Some say
John the Baptist, others say Elijah, and others Jeremiah or one of the prophets.' He said to them, 'But
who do you say that I am?' Simon Peter replied,
'You are the Christ, the Son of the living God.' And
Jesus answered him, 'Blessed are you, Simon Bar-
Jona! For flesh and blood has not revealed this to
you, but my Father who is in heaven. And I tell
you, you are Peter, and on this rock I will build my
church, and the powers of death shall not prevail
against it'" (Matt. 16:13-18).

After having verified that there was real faith
here, faith as a gift from the Father, the Lord went
on to speak about the "building" of his community.
Fellowship with him was to be a community of
believers.

The Hebrew word, **gahel,** which Jesus used for
"community" aroused in his hearers immediate men-
tal associations with the "community of Yahweh,"
the current formula in use among the Israelites
(Cf., for example, Deut. 23:1, 2, 3, 8; Judges 20:2).[7]
The Hebrew expression can best be paraphrased as
"assembled community." It also contains something
of the sense of our "meeting" or "togetherness."

This idea was particularly clearly expressed when the people of Israel gathered to praise or to entreat God: "I will tell of thy name to my brethren; in the midst of the congregation I will praise thee" (Ps. 22: 22; cf. also Ps. 26:12; 35:18; 40:9, 10; 89:7; 107:32). This unity was brought about by God himself when the Israelites formed the "assembly of Yahweh in the wilderness" (Num. 20:4; Acts 7:38), at the time when God brought the twelve tribes together and united them to form his people. The national community of Israel was Yahweh's possession, and therefore holy.

This community had clearly defined limits. The book of Deuteronomy sets out who belonged to it and who did not (Cf. Deut. 23:1-8). Its members formed a large family group and were called the "children of Israel" (cf., for example, Gen. 32:32) or the "house of Israel" (Acts 2:36). The Hebrew word used by Jesus was translated into Greek by words meaning "those called together" (**ekklesia**) and "those brought together" or "assembly" (**synagoge**). In the Greek New Testament, the term "those called to-gether" is applied to the Christian group and the term "those brought together" to the Jewish group. In English, the Christian group is usually known by the name "church," or "community," and the Jewish group by the name "synagogue." From the philo-logical point of view, this may be a purely fortuitous choice of words in the New Testament, but St. Paul's preference for the idea of being called together by God, and therefore for the word "church" (**ekklesia**),

cannot be denied. Christians are those "called into
the fellowship of the Son, Jesus Christ our Lord"
(1 Cor. 1:9; cf. also Rom. 8:30; Col. 3:15). The bond
between the church and the fact that Christians are
called together by God contributed more than any
other reason to the declaration that there was only
one Church, just as there was only one convocation,
or "calling together."[8]

The word "church," or "community," occurs 114
times in the New Testament, and is the usual title
given to the new community of Jesus. There is only
one case of its being used in the sense of an invisible
community or assembly and there (Heb. 12:23) it
refers to the heavenly Jerusalem. Elsewhere it always has the meaning of the visible community of
Christians, the continuation of the community of the
first Pentecost. It is used both for the local Christian
groups and generally also for the universal "Church
of God." This usage spread from Jerusalem to all
the local communities and goes back to the words of
the Lord himself. It is perhaps at first sight surprising that the phrase "the Church of God" is almost
always used, and, with one exception (Rom. 16:16),
the expression "the Church of Christ" never. The
reason for this is that the Christian community was
conscious of its being the new people of God, the
"Israel of God" (Gal. 6:16), the new fellowship
promised by the prophets of the Messiah and a
direct continuation of the community of ancient
Israel. God had made a "New Covenant" (cf. Matt.
26:28) with his new people, by the "blood of Christ,"

just as the Old Covenant had been made by the "blood of goats and calves" (Matt. 26:28; cf. also Heb. 9:12-22). "When Christ appeared as a high priest of the good things that have come" and "entered once for all into the Holy Place" (Heb. 9:11-12), the curtain of the temple, where the high priests of the Old Covenant offered sacrifices of expiation, "was torn in two, from top to bottom" (Matt. 15:38; Luke 23:45). While the paschal lambs were being slaughtered in the City for the annual feast celebrated in memory of the birth of the community of Yahweh, the "Lamb of God, who takes away the sins of the world" (John 1:29) was dying as "the surety of a better covenant" (Heb. 7:22). Finally, just as the Old Covenant was in the first place made and subsequently commemorated and confirmed every year by the sprinkling of blood and the partaking of a religious meal, so Jesus appointed his sacrificed body and blood to be food and drink in the New Covenant "in remembrance of him" (Exod. 24:5-6, 11; Mark 14:24; Luke 22:20; 1 Cor. 11:25). National or tribal relationship with Abraham was no longer the decisive factor, since God was able "from these stones to raise up children to Abraham" (Matt. 3:9). Although many of Abraham's descendants refused to acknowledge Christ, many were to come "from east and west and sit at table with Abraham, Isaac, and Jacob in the kingdom of heaven" because of their faith in him (Matt. 8:11; cf. also Luke 13:28-29; John 8:33-40) Not only Abraham's natural sons, but all who "follow the example of the faith of Abraham"

(Rom. 4:12) were Abraham's children (Cf. the whole of Rom. 4 and Heb. 11; Gal. 3:16-19; 4:21-31).

Jesus established what he called "My Community" as a direct extension of the "community of Yahweh." He enabled the validity of this new community to be apparent by giving it, among other things, the same foundation as that of the ancient community. The community of Yahweh had been built up on the basis of the twelve patriarchs, the sons of Jacob. The twelve tribes certainly grew more closely together, but the idea of twelve tribes survived within the community. The number twelve was a symbol of wholeness and completion. In the same way, Jesus also appointed twelve men, the "Twelve," as they were succinctly called from the beginning, to be the first generation of his community.[9] He himself pointed out this similarity between the old and the new communities, when Peter asked him what he and the other eleven men were to have for having followed him: "Truly, I say to you, in the new world, when the Son of man shall sit on his glorious throne, you who have followed me will also sit on twelve thrones, judging the twelve tribes of Israel" (Matt. 19:27-28; cf. also Luke 22:30). "Judging" here is an allusion to the guarantee and dispensation of justice and thus to ultimate salvation. Judging was regarded in Israel, as in the whole of the Ancient Near East, as one of the most important duties of a prince, with the result that "judge" often simply meant ruler (Amos 2:3) or was synonymous with king (Hos. 7:7; cf. also Judges 10:1, 3; 12:7, 9, 11, 14; 1 Kings 3:9; 2

Kings 15:5; Isa. 16:5; Ps. 2:10). Jesus was thus point-
ing out to the Twelve here their leading function in
the new Israel.[10] The symbolic meaning of the number twelve was clearly understood by the apostles —
their first independent action after the Lord's ascension was to choose a successor to Judas, who "was
numbered among us, and was allotted his share in
this ministry." With the consent of all those present, Peter said: "His office let another take. So one
of the men who have accompanied us during all the
time that the Lord Jesus went in and out among us
. . . must become with us a witness to his resurrection."
Matthias was chosen "to take the place in this ministry and apostleship from which Judas turned aside,"
and was thus "enrolled with the eleven apostles"
(Acts 1:15-26).

Thus the prophecy concerning the messianic time
was fulfilled. The Spirit of Yahweh descended, the
twelve tribes were united and the Messiah reigned
in their midst: "I will make a covenant of peace
with them; it shall be an everlasting covenant with
them; and I will bless them and multiply them, and
will set my sanctuary in the midst of them for ever-
more. My dwelling place shall be with them; and
I will be their God, and they shall be my people.
Then the nations will know that I, Yahweh, sanctify
Israel" (Ezek. 37:11-28).

This theme recurs in St. John's vision of the end
of time. He saw the new and eternal Jerusalem with
twelve gates inscribed with the names of the twelve
tribes of Israel and with twelve foundations bearing

the names of the twelve apostles: (Rev. 21:12, 14). It should be remembered in this connection that neither the gates nor the foundations of an ancient Near-Eastern city, built in a square, were regarded as independent entities in themselves, but only as forming part of the complete city wall. The individual significance of the names of the twelve tribes had virtually disappeared in Jesus' time — all that the twelve names did by this time was to indicate the wholeness of Israel. Jesus' intention, in using the number twelve in connection with the apostles, was undoubtedly to arouse a similar impression of his community.

The validity and the autonomy of the new community is also borne out by what would appear to be an incidental piece of information in the account of the election of Matthias. The company proposing the candidates for the office of the apostles "was in all about a hundred and twenty" persons (Acts 1:15). According to Jewish custom, this was the required number for any group wishing to appoint its own governing body. The probable meaning of this statement, then, is that the disciples were, as a special group within Israel, entitled to take this legal step.

It is clear from the second text in which Jesus uses the word "church" that he had a very concrete community in mind. In this text he regulates what we should call the discipline of the church. "If your brother sins against you, go and tell him his fault, between you and him alone. If he listens to you,

you have gained your brother. But if he does not listen, take one or two others along with you, that every word may be confirmed by the evidence of two or three witnesses. If he refuses to listen to them, tell it to the church; and if he refuses to listen even to the church, let him be to you as a Gentile and a tax collector" (Matt. 18:15-17). The last sentence is a clear indication of the limits of a distinct community, comparable to those of the synagogue, from which gentiles and sinners were similarly excluded. St. Paul put this into practice in the case of a public sinner: "Drive out this wicked person from among you" (1 Cor. 5:13; cf. also 2 John 7-11; 1 Tim. 1:19-20; 2 Thess. 3:14). This is comparable to his advice to Christians not to associate too closely with those who did not belong to the community of faith; here St. Paul reinforced his recommendation by a reference to the community of the Old Testament (2 Cor. 6:14; cf. also Eph. 5:7).

Jesus appointed responsible men to this new community — the "Twelve," chosen from among those who had been with him from the beginning (Cf. Acts 1:21). His first call inviting them to become his disciples had a more or less personal character, and others also joined him in response to this call. Seventy-two others are mentioned, whom he sent on "ahead of him, two by two, into every town and place where he himself was about to come" (Luke 10:1). After a while, however, the Twelve were specially called and appointed. This was an official and solemn event, following a whole night spent by Jesus in prayer. "And when it was day, he called his disciples, and chose from them twelve, whom he named apostles; Simon, whom he named Peter, and Andrew, his brother, and James and John, and Philip, and Bartholomew, and Matthew, and Thomas, and James the son of Alphaeus, and Simon who was called the Zealot, and Judas (the brother) of James, and Judas Iscariot, who became a traitor" (Luke 6:12-16; cf. also Matt. 10:1-4; Mark 3:13-19).

Jesus called them "apostles." The original Greek word acquired from Jesus a very special meaning which it did not possess either in secular Greek usage or in the Greek writings of the early Jews, namely envoy, witness or messenger. "And he appointed twelve, to be with him, and to be sent out to preach and have authority to cast out demons" (Mark 3:14). The function of the envoy acquired a juridical significance from the Aramaic word used by Jesus, so that it meant "representative with full powers," since, according to ancient Semitic law, a person's envoy acted legally as the person himself. The apostles were thus witnesses "representing" the Lord in places where he himself was not physically present, and especially during the period after his return to the Father. This accounts for the fact that, after a transitory commission (Mark 6:7-11, 30), after which they were once again called "disciples," their function did not come into operation until after the ascension of the Lord and the descent of the Holy Spirit.

The mission on which the apostles were sent was,

however, not of a purely legal nature. It was much more than that, since the Lord himself intended to be present through them among "all nations," preaching, baptizing, binding and loosing, "to the close of the age" (Matt. 28:20). From the moment that the Lord was at the right hand of the Father and had sent his Holy Spirit down to them, it was the apostles who built up Christ's community and kept it together, and formed the "foundation" of the Church (Eph. 2:20). Jesus sent them, as he himself had been sent by the Father. On the eve of his resurrection, he said to them: "As the Father has sent me, even so I send you" (John 20:21), and thus: "He who receives you receives me, and he who receives me receives him who sent me" (Matt. 10:40) and "He who hears you hears me, and he who rejects you rejects me, and he who rejects me rejects him who sent me" (Luke 10:16).

As the authentic representatives of the Lord, the apostles were also able to perform signs and miracles in his name, signs characteristic of the Messiah and his work: "Preach as you go, saying, 'The kingdom of heaven is at hand.' Heal the sick, raise the dead, cleanse lepers, cast out demons" (Matt. 10:7-8). And indeed, "many wonders and signs were done through the apostles" (Acts 2:43; cf. also 4:30; 5:12; Rom. 15:18-19; Heb. 2:2-4; 2 Cor. 12:12). It was the Lord himself who spoke in the words of the apostles: "Those who received his (Peter's) word were baptized" and thus "the Lord added to their number day by day those who were being saved" (Acts 2:41, 47).

The apostles "went forth and preached everywhere, while the Lord worked with them and confirmed the message by the signs that attended it" (Mark 16:19). They were aware that they were sent in Christ's name: "We are ambassadors for Christ, God making his appeal through us. We beseech you on behalf of Christ, be reconciled to God" (2 Cor. 5:20; cf. also 2:17; 13:3; 1 Thess. 2:13).

Jesus himself formulated the apostles' authoritative mission as his representatives in the Church with the emphatic statement: "Truly, I say to you, whatever you bind on earth shall be bound in heaven, and whatever you loose on earth shall be loosed in heaven" (Matt. 18:18). "Binding and loosing" was a phrase well known to those who heard Jesus; it was a rabbinical formula, and almost a technical term, referring in the first place to the right and the duty to exclude certain people from, or to allow them to be admitted again into the temple or the synagogue. It was also applied to doctrinal and legal questions and in such cases had the meaning of authoritatively declaring, forbidding or admitting. The Twelve were thus appointed as the authoritative leaders of the Church, with the task of keeping the community of Jesus together and defining its limits by means of doctrinal and disciplinary decisions. In this way, they were similar to those who held authority in Israel and carried out a parallel function.

Just before his ascension, Jesus once again summarized the task and the plenary powers of the apostles in the solemn formula: "All authority in heaven and on earth has been given to me. Go therefore and make disciples of all nations, baptizing them in the name of the Father and of the Son and of the Holy Spirit, teaching them to observe all that I have commanded you" (Matt. 28:16-20). He had already instructed them, on the eve of the sacrifice of the New Covenant, to give thanks over the bread and the chalice "in remembrance of me" (Luke 22:19). He had also given them, on the day of his resurrection, full powers of binding and loosing: "If you forgive the sins of any, they are forgiven; if you retain the sins of any, they are retained" (John 20:22).

The task which the Twelve received from the Lord consisted therefore of representing him in the midst of his community and, from the center of this community, before the world. Jesus himself stood behind their words, their administration of the sacrament and their conduct of affairs. After giving them the task of baptizing, preaching to and leading all peoples, he told them: "Lo, I am with you always, to the close of the age" (Matt. 28:20). To enable them to carry out this task, he promised them his Holy Spirit: "He (the Father) will give you another Counsellor, to be with you for ever, even the Spirit of truth, whom the world cannot receive, because it neither sees him nor knows him; you know him, for he dwells with you, and will be in you, the Counsellor, the Holy Spirit, whom the Father will send in my name, he will teach you all things, and bring to your remembrance all that I have said to you"; "When the Spirit of truth comes, he will guide you into the truth; for he will not speak on his own authority, but whatever he hears he will speak, and he will declare to you the things that are to come. He will glorify me, for he will take what is mine and declare it to you" (John 14:17, 26; 16:13-14).

When Jesus was already on the way back to his Father, on the day of his resurrection, this promise was beginning to be fulfilled. He appeared to the eleven apostles, breathed over them and said: "Receive the Holy Spirit" (John 20:22). The full, public descent of the Spirit of the Lord took place on the Feast of Pentecost. From that moment onward, the apostles went out and began to gather round them "all that are far off, every one whom the Lord our God calls to him" (Acts 2:39; cf. also Eph. 2:13, 17; 1 Pet. 2:9). It was therefore through the Holy Spirit dwelling in them and teaching them all truth, that Jesus kept them together. "There are varieties of gifts, but the same Spirit; and there are varieties of service, but the same Lord; and there are varieties of working, but it is the same God who inspires them all in every one" — there were, then, to be many different ministers and ministries within the one "apostolic community" in and through which the Lord would guide all men and instruct them in all things, though no longer in a directly physical manner, but "all these are inspired by one and the same Spirit, who apportions to each one individually as he wills" (1 Cor. 12:4-6, 11).

An essential aspect, therefore, of Jesus' community, is that, throughout the time beginning with the ascension and ending with the Lord's Second Coming, it is guided both by the Holy Spirit and by the apostles. The Spirit of the Lord is the guarantee of the unity of the community, and the office of the apostles provides the form of its unity. This office was moreover bound to continue in this form after the death of the Twelve. In this way, the one Shepherd continues to feed his one flock.

The apostolic office began its task when the Lord ascended and the Holy Spirit descended. From that time forward, the Twelve were called the "apostles," although they continued to be known, as a general rule, as the "disciples." It was from that moment that their appearance "in Jesus' name" commenced — their preaching, baptizing, binding and loosing, and their celebration of the memorial of "the Lord's death until he comes" (1 Cor. 11:26). The task of the apostolic office will, however, automatically come to an end again at the Lord's Second Coming. Jesus himself makes reference in his parables to such people as "stewards" and "envoys" who have the task of looking after their masters' affairs until the master's return. It is also clear, from this reference to the Return of the Lord, that in certain respects the office of the apostles was to be continued after the death of the Twelve. Even while the Twelve were still alive, certain men appeared who had a special function to fulfill in the service of this office. There were the "elders" or "presbyters" who had a collegial executive function in accordance with

the Jewish tradition (Acts 11:30; 14:23; Titus 1:5;
James 5:14; 1 Pet. 5:1). There were also the "over-
seers" or "leaders" whose office was that of an "episco-
pate" — they were the **episcopi** or bishops whose
function was probably no different from that of the
elders (Phil. 1:1; 1 Tim. 3:1-7). Finally, there were
also the deacons whose duties were both spiritual
and material (Acts 6:1-6; 8:5-13, 38; 1 Tim. 3:8-13).
Those who had to appear as responsible leaders after
the death of the Twelve were not, however, given
the same authority as those first witnesses who were
able to testify from their own seeing and hearing.
They were not personally appointed by Jesus himself
and they were not to have the same personal charism
of infallibility. Wherever the Twelve had appeared
as founders of a community within the Church, the
ministers of the apostolic office who followed them
had the task of maintaining this church and of keeping it true to itself. There is, then, a distinction between the "office of the apostles," which is unique
and cannot be repeated, and the "apostolic office" in
the more restricted sense of a service continuing
the fundamental and permanently conclusive work
of the Twelve. The task of the successors to the
Twelve was to keep Jesus' community together on
the "foundation of the apostles" (Eph. 2:20; cf. also
1 Cor. 3:10-17). When the apostles proceeded to
appoint helpers and men to continue their work
(cf. for example, Acts 14:22-23), they referred to
the norm of apostolic preaching: "This charge I com-
mit to you, Timothy, . . . that inspired by them
(the prophetic utterances) you may wage the good

warfare, holding faith and a good conscience. By rejecting conscience, certain persons have made shipwreck of their faith"; "O Timothy, guard what has been entrusted to you" (1 Tim. 1:18-19; 6:20); "Follow the pattern of the sound words which you have heard from me; . . . guard the truth that has been entrusted to you by the Holy Spirit who dwells in us" (2 Tim. 1:13-14). Timothy too was to pass on this task to others: "What you have heard from me before many witnesses entrust to faithful men who will be able to teach others also" (2 Tim. 2:2). The last of these texts refers to the many links in the chain of those to hold ecclesiastical office — the long series of men connecting the Church of the first Pentecost with that of the Lord's Second Coming. Christians were urged: "Obey your leaders and submit to them; for they are keeping watch over your souls, as men who will have to give account. Let them do this joyfully, and not sadly, for that would be of no advantage to you" (Heb. 13:17). The apostle Paul asked Christians "to respect those who labor among you and are over you in the Lord and admonish you, and to esteem them very highly in love because of their work" (1 Thess. 5:12-13). The first converts in Achaia, who subsequently entered the service of the community, prompted him to say: "I urge you to be subject to such men and to every fellow worker and laborer" (1 Cor. 16:16). In this way, the unity of Jesus' community was to be preserved throughout time and Jesus' promise, to be with the apostles "always, to the close of the age" (Matt. 28:20) and to send his Spirit to be with them "for ever" (John 14:16) was to be fulfilled.

The unity of the community is to be found in the one Lord. He is always present in it throughout its pilgrimage, invisibly through his Holy Spirit and visibly through his "representatives." The unity of the community in Christ and in his Spirit is thus apparent in the "apostolic Church." Concerning the Word of life, we have been instructed "by his holy apostles and prophets in the Spirit" (Eph. 3:5) and by the baptism of the apostles "in one Spirit we were all baptized into one body" (1 Cor. 12:13), so that, being "built upon the foundation of the apostles and prophets, Christ Jesus himself being the cornerstone," we are kept together as one whole structure in him and "grow into a holy temple in the Lord," thus becoming "a dwelling place of God in the Spirit" (Eph. 2:20-22).

5

THE HOUSE ON THE ROCK

When he instituted the apostolic office, Jesus gave a visible shape to his community for the time during which he was to be physically absent from it. In order to reveal the unity that he had given to the Church through his Spirit as a visible manifestation and to enable this unity to function, he appointed one of the Twelve to be their official central point. Just as Israel right up to the time of Jesus recognized the "seat of Moses," from which the scribes and pharisees were able, according to the testimony of the Lord, to teach authoritatively (Matt. 23:2-3), so did the new Israel receive what traditionally came to be known as the "Chair of Peter." This was in no sense a new office ranking higher than that of the apostles, but an appointment within the body of the apostles with the function of keeping this body together. Jesus' first words to Simon, when his brother Andrew had brought him to Jesus, were: "So you are Simon, the son of John? You shall be called Cephas, which means Peter" (John 1:42). The evangelists frequently mention "Simon, whom he surnamed Peter," or "Simon, whom he named Peter" (cf., for example, Mark 3:16; Luke 6:14), and Paul never calls him Simon, but always Peter or Cephas

(Cf. for example, Gal. 1:18; 2:11; 1 Cor. 1:12; 3:22).
This use of the word as the name of a person was
quite new. Neither **Cephas** in Aramaic nor **Petros** in
Greek (the Latin form of which was **Petrus,** the
English, **Peter**) had been employed as such before
Jesus' time. The Aramaic word used by Jesus meant
a rock or stony ground. This meaning was not immediately discernible in the Latin **Petrus** and only
partly in the Greek **Petros.** It is only the French
Pierre which is used to designate both a person and
a stone. In changing Simon's name to Peter, Jesus
wished to express beforehand the special task which
he was later to give to this disciple. His intention
was not lost upon those who heard him do this, for
had God not given a new name to Abram, Sarai and
Jacob, with the purpose of expressing their special
function in the history of salvation? (Cf. Gen. 17:5;
17:16; 35:10). They were acquainted with the many
significant names of persons and places in Israel and
with the phrase: "As his name is, so is he" (1 Sam.
25:25).

The Lord explained the meaning of this change
of name some time afterwards. After having ques-
tioned his disciples about their thoughts on the subject of the Son of Man, and after Peter's confession
of faith, Jesus turned to him and said: "Blessed are
you, Simon Bar-Jona! For flesh and blood has not
revealed this to you, but my Father who is in heaven.
And I tell you, you are Peter, and on this rock I
will build my church, and the powers of death shall
not prevail against it" (Matt. 16:17-18). The Lord

compared his community to a house, and the foundation of this house recalled his parable of the "wise man who built his house upon the rock; and the rain fell, and the floods came, and the winds blew and beat upon that house, but it did not fall, because it had been founded on the rock" (Matt. 7:24-25; Luke 6:48). A firm foundation enables a house to continue to stand. In the same way, Peter was given the task of holding up the apostles and thereby the whole community of the Church. This image, in which the Church is compared to a house, occurs frequently in the New Testament. Peter, for example, called Christ the keystone, the stone "which has become the head of the corner" (Acts 4:11), the chief element in the construction on which the whole house depended. St. Paul also used the same image when he referred to James, Cephas and John as "pillars" of the house of the Church in the community of Jerusalem (Gal. 2:9). "We are his house" (Heb. 3:6), "the household of God, which is the church of the living God" (1 Tim. 3:15; 1 Pet. 4:17), "from living stones built into a spiritual house" (1 Pet. 2:4) and "God's temple" in which "God's Spirit dwells" (1 Cor. 3:16).

The words which immediately follow Jesus' statement concerning Peter as the rock upon which he was to build his Church provide an explanatory comment upon Peter's task: "I will give you the keys of the kingdom of heaven, and whatever you bind on earth shall be bound in heaven, and whatever you loose on earth shall be loosed in heaven" (Matt.

16:19). In Israel, the keys of a house belonged exclusively to the master of that house. In his absence, he would entrust these keys to the steward or major-domo; in so doing, he handed over to this person the responsibility for the management of the household affairs and for the upkeep of the house. The Messiah was the Lord of his house, the Church, and it was he who had control of the keys — "He shall open, and none shall shut; and he shall shut, and none shall open" (Isa. 22:22; cf. also Apoc. 3:7). It was said of the rabbis that they too had control of keys, namely the "key of knowledge" (Luke 11:52), and thus had the power to unlock the sacred books for others to be able to hear the word of God. In giving Peter the key of his house, the Church, Jesus appointed him as his steward, to be in charge of the house during the time that he was with his Father until the moment of his return. The handing over of the key did not make Peter the owner of the house, but its major-domo. His task was to preserve everything that the Lord had established in the house. He had the authority to make everything function in the household exactly as the Lord had ordained, and to open or to shut the door to people in accordance with his Lord's commission.

Jesus also gave the other apostles the power to "bind and loose," and from this it is clear that they were Peter's fellow apostles, though Peter, the Rock, or the man with the power of the keys, was the one authorized to preside over the Twelve and to co-ordinate the activities of the group. It was he too who had to be a help and support to "his brothers" at critical moments. Just before his passion, the Lord said to him: "Simon, Simon, behold, Satan demanded to have you, that he might sift you like wheat, but I have prayed for you that your faith may not fail; and when you have turned again, strengthen your brethren" (Luke 22:31-32).

Between his resurrection and his ascension, Jesus took Peter to one side, apart from the other apostles, in order that he, as the "Shepherd of his flock," might entrust his sheep to Peter. "Jesus said to Simon Peter, 'Simon, son of John, do you love me more than these?' He said to him, 'Yes, Lord; you know that I love you.' He said to him, 'Feed my lambs.' A second time he said to him, 'Simon, son of John, do you love me?' He said to him, 'Yes, Lord; you know that I love you.' He said to him, 'Tend my sheep.' He said to him the third time, 'Simon, son of John, do you love me?' Peter was grieved because he said to him the third time, 'Do you love me?' And he said to him, 'Lord, you know everything; you know that I love you.' Jesus said to him, 'Feed my sheep' " (John 21:15-17).

If a flock is to remain together, it can have no more than one shepherd. As Peter himself wrote at a later stage, Jesus was the "chief Shepherd" who was to appear again at the end (1 Pet. 5:4). Jesus was "the Shepherd and Guardian of your souls" (1 Pet. 2:25), whereas Peter was his "servant and apostle" (2 Pet. 1:1). Jesus entrusted the faithful to Peter as "my" sheep, and Peter refers to them in his epistles as the "flock of God" (1 Pet. 5:2). Peter was

to act as the community's shepherd in Jesus' name,
and the unity of the flock was to be perceptible and
to be experienced in his office as that of the one
Shepherd.

Jesus repeated his commission to Peter to act in his
name as the community's shepherd three times. This
in the first place served to emphasize the solemn
nature of his commission. It is also probable that
it contained an allusion to Peter's later threefold
denial of his Lord: (John 18:17, 25, 27). Finally,
Jesus may also have been following an ancient Near
Eastern legal practice which went back to the time
of Abraham and which is still common today in that
part of the world. It was customary, and indeed
necessary, for a declaration which conferred certain
rights or privileges to be made three times in the
presence of witnesses, if the statement were to have
absolute validity. It is understandable that such a
ceremony should be practiced in a society which
depended for its legal security on the spoken word,
heard by those present, and not on the written word
or on documents.[11]

Although Peter's office did not commence until
the Lord had returned to the Father, Peter already
played a very prominent part during the time that
Jesus was still on earth. His name occurs more than
a hundred times in the four gospels alone, whereas
none of the other apostles is mentioned more than
thirty times. His is the first name to appear in the
four lists of the apostles provided by the Bible. With
the exception of Judas, the traitor, who is always

named last, the names of the other apostles, on the other hand, are listed in a different order (Cf. Matt. 10:2; Mark 3:16; Luke 6:14; Acts 1:13). Peter's special position is particularly emphasized in St. Matthew's gospel: "First, Simon, who is called Peter." He accompanied the Lord everywhere, and witnessed all his signs. With John and James, he was one of the privileged three allowed to be present at the raising of Jairus' daughter (Mark 5:37; Luke 8:51), at the transfiguration on the mountain (Matt. 17:1; Mark 9:2; Luke 9:28), and at the agony in the Garden of Olives: (Matt. 26:37; Mark 14:33).

Peter was usually the spokesman for the group, as, for example, after the miraculous catch of fish when Jesus set out in Peter's boat (Luke 5:3, 10), at the end of the sermon on the Eucharist (John 6:68), at the payment of the temple tax (Matt. 17:24 f.), when the Lord was questioning the apostles about their faith in the Son of Man (Matt. 16:16), during the washing of the feet at the time of the last supper (John 13:6-10), on those occasions when an explanation of the meaning of a parable was sought (Matt. 15:15; Luke 12:41), at the Lord's transfiguration (Matt. 17:4), when the woman with a flow of blood was cured (Luke 8:45) and in the case of the believer's duty to forgive others (Matt. 18:21). The phrase "Simon (Peter) and those who were with him" (Mark 1:36; Luke 9:32) should therefore cause no surprise, nor should the fact that outsiders, such as the tax-collectors, applied to Peter for his Master's contribution (Matt. 17:24). Finally, the character of

this apostle emerges with exceptional clarity from
the references in the gospels to his shortcomings.

After Jesus had risen from the dead, the news of
his resurrection was taken to "his disciples and
Peter" (Mark 16:7), or to "Simon Peter and the other
disciple whom Jesus loved" (John 20:2), and Peter
was the first to enter the empty tomb in order to
verify what had happened with his own eyes and
then "the other disciple, who reached the tomb first,
also went in" (John 20:2-8; cf. also Luke 24:12).
The risen Lord appeared separately to Peter before
showing himself to the whole group of the apostles
(Luke 24:34; 1 Cor. 15:5), and the apostles believed
Peter's testimony and said to those who were on the
way to Emmaus: "The Lord has risen indeed, and
has appeared to Simon."

There is only one reference in the gospels to
Peter's acting on his own initiative during the period
between the resurrection and the ascension of the
Lord: "Simon Peter said to them, 'I am going fish-
ing.' They said to him, 'We will go with you'"
(John 21:3). After the ascension, however, it is clear
from numerous passages and references that the
apostles understood Jesus' appointment of Peter.
Luke, the author of the Acts of the Apostles, for
example no longer refers to him as "Simon, whom
he named Peter," as he had done in his gospel, but
simply as "Peter."

When the apostles were assembled after the ascension in the upper room with a group of disciples,
Peter emerged as their leader in connection with

the first question to be settled, namely that of the
choice of a successor to Judas Iscariot (Acts 1:15-26).
It was Peter who made the first declaration of the
young Church after the spectacular descent of the
Holy Spirit and acted as spokesman for the Jewish
people, surrounded by the eleven (Acts 2:14; cf.
also 2:38; 5:29). It was he, too, who spoke after the
healing of the man, who had been lame from birth,
in the temple (Acts 3) and who fearlessly addressed
the Council of the Jews (Acts 4:1-22; 5:29-32). He
defended the holiness of the Church and pronounced
God's judgment on Ananias and Sapphira (Acts
5:1-11). It was he who visited the Christian communities in Judea, Samaria and Galilee (Acts 8:14-25;
9:32; 10:23) and addressed himself in his first epistle
to the faithful in Pontus, Galatia, Cappadocia, Asia
and Bithynia, districts into which the Church had
spread mainly as a result of the preaching of St.
Paul (1 Pet. 1:1).

The only definite miraculous signs recorded are
those performed by Peter. These are the healing of
the lame man in the temple (Acts 3:1-8), the curing
of Aeneas in Lydda (Acts 9:33-35) and the bringing
to life of the girl Tabitha in Joppa (Acts 9:36-43).
The account of the last-named event bears a striking
resemblance to the raising of Jairus' daughter by
Jesus himself (Luke 8:49-56). The chief difference
is, however, that St. Luke records that Peter prayed
before performing the miracle. It is clear from the
fact that the sick were brought to Peter, as they
had previously been brought to Jesus, that Peter

was regarded even by outsiders as the one who represented Christ in the midst of the community in a very special way. It is reported in the Acts that "they even carried out the sick into the streets, and laid them on beds and pallets, that as Peter came by at least his shadow might fall on some of them. The people also gathered from the towns around Jerusalem, bringing the sick and those affected with unclean spirits, and they were all healed" (Acts 5:14-16; cf. also Mark 6:56; Luke 4:40). In the eyes of the people, it was Peter who had received the prophet's mantle from Jesus, as Elisha before him had received the mantle from Elijah.

After Peter had decided to receive the first Jewish converts at the first, miraculous feast of Pentecost (Acts 2:38), he also became the first to receive gentiles into the community. The Lord himself urged him to take this step in a vision and by sending the Holy Spirit down upon the gentiles who were listening to Peter's sermon (Acts 10). Peter was able to defend his action when his brethren reproached him with it on his return to Jerusalem. On his initiative, a new period had been initiated in the history of the Church (Acts 11:1-18). The conditions under which gentiles were permitted to join the Christian community, which had, for the first few years, consisted exclusively of believers of Jewish origin, were, however, the cause of violent contention within the Church. Again it was Peter who made the decisive speech that was accepted by all the apostles and elders present at the council of Jerusalem which had been summoned for the purpose of considering this question in the year 49 or 50 A.D. "And after there had been much debate, Peter rose and said to them, 'Brethren, you know that in the early days God made a choice among you, that by my mouth the Gentiles should hear the word of the gospel and believe. And God who knows the heart bore witness to them, giving them the Holy Spirit just as he did to us; and he made no distinction between us and them, but cleansed their hearts by faith. Now therefore why do you make trial of God by putting a yoke upon the neck of the disciples which neither our fathers nor we have been able to bear? But we believe that we shall be saved through the grace of the Lord Jesus, just as they will.' And all the assembly kept silence" (Acts 15:7-12).

The importance of this decision and Peter's authority, as exemplified in his decision and its reception by the Council, is also powerfully borne out by Paul's rebuke of Peter at Antioch. It had been decided at Jerusalem that it was not necessary for Christians of gentile origin to observe the Jewish laws, but at the same time it had been requested that they should adapt themselves to the practice of the Jewish Christians of abstaining from what had been strangled, from blood and from flesh from the gentile temples. Peter later met a group of Christians of gentile origin in Antioch, and ate with them without any regard for the Jewish dietary laws. When a party of Jewish Christians arrived, however, these men took their meals separately and thus observed

the Jewish laws. What Peter did had been permitted by the Council of Jerusalem, and what the
group of Jewish Christians did had also not been
forbidden by the Council. When Peter subsequently
left the gentile group and "separated himself, fearing
the circumcision party," Paul "opposed him to his face,
because he stood condemned" (Gal. 2:11-13). Paul,
was not opposed to the fact that the Jewish Christians
observed the Jewish laws; he was merely protesting
against the fact that Peter had done this, since he,
in view of his exceptional position, could scarcely
"compel the Gentiles to live like Jews," while he,
"though a Jew, lived like a Gentile and not like a
Jew" (Gal. 2:15).

The event described above throws light not only
on the exceptional position occupied even outside
Jerusalem by Peter, but also on the fact that he had
to lead the Church together with the other apostles.
Not only he, but the whole body of the apostles
formed the "foundation" of the Church (Eph. 2:20).
The Twelve were "fellow-disciples" in each others'
presence, and Peter wrote to the elders, the leaders
of individual communities, referring to himself as "a
fellow elder" (1 Pet. 5:1) and to Paul as "our beloved
brother" (2 Pet. 3:15). Peter was the first in a circle
of "brothers," and the task of preaching, baptizing,
celebrating the Eucharist and of binding and loosing
was extended to the entire body of the apostles, just
as the Holy Spirit had been promised and given
to the whole group. Peter had, however, been given
the task of keeping them together, of "consolidating"

them, of holding the key to the house, the Church, and of being the specially appointed shepherd of the Lord's sheep. Peter's office is inconceivable without that of his fellow-apostles, but it formed the visible and authoritative central point, giving shape and form to their unity in Christ and his Spirit and enabling it to function effectively.

The Church received the office of Peter from her Lord so that she might experience, preserve and show to the world her unity in a fully human manner — "so that the world may know that thou (the Father) hast sent me (the Son) and hast loved them even as thou hast loved me" (John 17:23). The Church is unable to do without this guarantee, this sign of "perfect unity" (John 17:23), and that is why, when Peter had been imprisoned, "earnest prayer was made for him to God by the church" (Acts 12:5, 12). It is also why it was the Lord himself who freed him and gave him back to the Church (Acts 12:17).

By instituting the office of Peter, the Lord completed the unity of the apostolic structure of his community. Peter and the eleven might eventually die, but the Lord would carry on with his activity through their office "to the close of the age" (Matt. 28:26), promising his Spirit to the Twelve "for ever" (John 14:16). There would be "faithful men who will be able to teach others also" (2 Tim. 2:2) until his Second Coming, men with the gift received by prophecy when the elders laid their hands upon them (Cf. 1 Tim. 4:14). As Peter had received the pastoral office and had passed it on to others, to whom he wrote "Tend the flock of God that is your charge," so would there always be shepherds who would protect and keep the sheep together until "the chief Shepherd is manifested" (1 Pet. 5:2, 4).

6

UNITY IN THE SERVICE OF
ONE'S BROTHERS

The words and deeds of the Lord, as narrated by St. John in his account of the Last Supper, form the core of this most subtly penetrating of the four gospels. Jesus was face to face with his "hour." The decisive moment in the fulfillment of his mission had come. All that he did and said in the presence of the Twelve at this time was full of his longing to complete his mission. And this mission was to reconcile and to unite — to unite himself with his own, to unite his own among themselves in him and to unite himself with his own in the Father. "His hour had come" and he was now, by dying, to bring this unity into the world. On this, the eve of his death, he was bound to bear witness to this sacred unity.

His testimony had to express the inexpressible — a great multitude of thoughts and feelings. He therefore chose one of the most concrete and direct aspects of this new unity and communicated it to his own in an unforgettable symbolic action.

"Now when Jesus knew that his hour had come to depart out of this world to the Father, having loved

his own who were in the world, he loved them to
the end. . . . Jesus, knowing that the Father had
given all things into his hands, and that he had come
from God and was going to God, rose from supper,
laid aside his garments, and girded himself with a
towel. Then he poured water into a basin, and began
to wash the disciples' feet, and to wipe them with
the towel with which he was girded. He came to
Simon Peter; and Peter said to him, 'Lord, do you
wash my feet?' Jesus answered him, 'What I am
doing you do not know now, but afterwards you will
understand.' Peter said to him, 'You shall never
wash my feet.' Jesus answered him, 'If I do not
wash you, you have no part in me.' Simon Peter
said to him, 'Lord, not my feet only but also my
hands and my head!' Jesus said to him, 'He who
has bathed does not need to wash, except for his
feet, but he is clean all over; and you are clean,
but not all of you.' For he knew who was to betray
him; that was why he said, 'You are not all clean.'
When he had washed their feet, and taken his garments, and resumed his place, he said to them, 'Do
you know what I have done to you? You call me
Teacher and Lord; and you are right, for so I am.
If I then, your Lord and Teacher, have washed your
feet, you also ought to wash one another's feet. For
I have given you an example, that you also should
do as I have done to you. Truly, truly, I say to you,
a servant is not greater than his master; nor is he
who is sent greater than he who sent him. If you
know these things, blessed are you if you do them'"
(John 13:1-17).

The unity between Jesus and his own arose from his readiness to serve: "The Son of Man came not to be served, but to serve" (Matt. 20:28; Mark 10:45). In this service, Jesus emerged from himself and approached his own. Similarly, in serving each other, men open themselves to each other. The human community is born in mutual service. Thus God, who has need of no one and who is sufficient, and indeed more than sufficient, to himself, opened himself to men, giving them existence and access to him. Man rejected this existence with God, this life side by side with God, and yielded to the temptation to "be like God" (Gen. 3:5), to be sufficient to himself and to acknowledge no partner, saying, "I will not serve" (Jer. 2:20). Man became estranged from God and from his fellow-men by becoming completely centered in himself. He maintained this isolation by asserting himself and prevailing over his fellows and by looking to no one and tolerating nothing that did not belong to him.

God reconciled us with himself by sending his Son to us in "the form of a servant" (Phil. 2:7). The Son of Man appeared among us as the "servant of Yahweh" who was to accomplish "the will of Yahweh" (Isa. 52:13; 53:10). Yahweh's servant was at the same time our servant: "He has borne our griefs and carried our sorrows; . . . he was wounded for our transgressions, he was bruised for our iniquities" (Isa. 53:4-5). Jesus was both God and Man. A double readiness to serve was therefore revealed in him. First, God, whom all men were seeking, the

Israelites and the gentiles together, revealed himself
in God the Son: "And now Yahweh says, who formed
me from the womb to be his servant, to bring Jacob
back to him, and that Israel might be gathered to
him, . . . 'It is too light a thing that you should be my
servant to raise up the tribes of Jacob and to restore
the preserved of Israel; I will give you as a light to the
nations, that my salvation may reach to the end of
the earth . . . I have kept you and given you as a
covenant to the people, to establish the land, . . .
saying to the prisoners, Come forth, and to those
who are in darkness, Appear' " (Isa. 49:5-6, 8-9).
Therefore he "who among you fears Yahweh" should
"obey the voice of his servant," and he "who walks
in darkness and has no light" should "trust in the
name of Yahweh and rely upon his God" (Isa. 1:10).
Secondly, the Man who was ready to serve God was
also revealed in Jesus, "who, though he was in the
form of God, did not count equality with God a
thing to be grasped, but emptied himself, taking the
form of a servant, being born in the likeness of men.
And being found in human form he humbled himself and became obedient unto death, even death on
a cross" (Phil. 2:6-8). God thus brought about our
redemption and it was accepted from God's hand by
us in rendering service.

Jesus' washing of the disciples' feet, and his per-
formance of this action in the manner and in the
clothing of a servant, was more than a vivid and
concrete instruction on the subject of man's need
to help his fellows in society. He revealed in the

washing of the feet the manner in which God's reconciliation with men and man's reconciliation with
his fellows was to be brought about according to
the divine plan of salvation. It meant, in other words,
that man must place himself at God's disposal, that
he must sincerely wish to be both God's and his
brothers' servant and to live according to God's intention that he should constantly be turned towards
his fellows. We were created for this and we are
redeemed by it. We must lose our lives if we are to
find them (Cf. Luke 9:24; 17:33).

This way of looking at things struck those who
were still unredeemed and unenlightened as strange,
and they could have, in Jesus' own words, no part
in him, no fellowship with him (Cf. John 13:8). Different standards applied in human society in this
world, and that is why the world was unable to give
real peace (Cf. John 14:27). The disciples too needed
time to become completely steeped in Jesus' vision.
The gospels record that the mother of two of them,
James and John, requested that they should be given
a position of special importance. Jesus, however,
summoned the Twelve and told them: "You know
that the rulers of the Gentiles lord it over them, and
their great men exercise authority over them. It shall
not be so among you; but whoever would be great
among you must be your servant, and whoever would
be first among you must be your slave; even as the
Son of Man came not to be served but to serve"
(Matt. 20:20-28; cf. also Mark 10:35-45). Even at the
beginning of the Last Supper, there was disagree-

ment among the Twelve as to who should take
precedence at table. Once again, Jesus affirmed:
"The kings of the Gentiles exercise lordship over
them; and those in authority over them are called
benefactors. But not so with you; rather let the
greatest among you become as the youngest, and
the leader as one who serves. For which is the
greater, one who sits at table, or one who serves?
Is it not the one who sits at table? But I am among
you as one who serves" (Luke 22:24-27).

Office in the Church is, then, essentially different
from a position of worldly authority. The apostles
and the other leaders in Jesus' community spontaneously called themselves the "servants of God" (Acts
4:29; 16:17; Titus 1:1; James 1:1; Apoc. 10:7), the
"servants of Jesus Christ" (Rom. 1:1; Eph. 6:6; Phil.
1:1; Col. 4:12; Jude 1; Apoc. 1:1), the "slaves to all"
(1 Cor. 10:19) or "your servants" (2 Cor. 4:5). This
was not a literary convention. It was an exact desig-
nation of everyone working within the Church. Anyone receiving an office in the Church was at the
same time given a task in the service of God, of
Christ and of his brothers. The Greek word normally
used for office in the Bible is **diakonia,** which means
the rendering of services or duties performed in
service. Terms such as "office," "authority" and
"power" do occur in the New Testament, but they
are used only in connection with persons holding
positions in civil life or in the synagogue, or with
the angelic powers, and never in connection with
those holding positions in the Church.[12] In the ac-

count of the appointment of the deacons, this term, **diakonia** or "official duties," is used both for service at table and for the service of God's word in preaching (Acts 6:1-4). Preaching was, then, an official duty both in respect of God and of his Word and in respect of the community. But the other offices in the Church were also "official duties" **(diakonia)**: "There are varieties of service" (1 Cor. 12:5), and the Lord appointed some to be "apostles, some prophets, some evangelists, some pastors and teachers, for the equipment of the saints, for the work of the ministry **(diakonia)**, for the building up of the body of Christ" (Eph. 4:11-12, Greek text). Those who hold office in the Church are, in other words, dedicated "to the service of the saints" (1 Cor. 16:15).

The various functions in Christ's community are not given to men to enable them to make a successful career for themselves or to achieve an honorable position or a high rank commensurate to their social status. They form rather a "ministry of reconciliation" (2 Cor. 5:18) and as such must be carried out, as the Lord himself carried out his functions, in an attitude which is "gentle and lowly in heart" (Matt. 11:19). Anyone who ceases to regard his office in the Church as a service to his brothers is bound to do violence to this ministry of reconciliation, to cause the unity of Christ's community to lose its luster and even perhaps seriously to endanger this unity. Unity in Christ was brought about by the sacrifice, the giving away of himself of the "Servant of Yahweh," and a similar sacrifice is required of all those who are called to this unity.

After washing the disciples' feet, Jesus sent Judas away. Judas did not understand the meaning of Jesus' action. He had chosen himself and refused to serve and consequently had no part in Jesus. When he had gone, Jesus told the others: "A new commandment I give you, that you love one another; even as I have loved you, that you also love one another. By this all men will know that you are my disciples, if you have love for one another" (John 13:34-35).

This mutual love is not simply **one** of many marks of Christ's Church. It is **the** mark of the Church. In his prayer towards the end of, or after the Last Supper, Jesus returned to this theme: "That they may all be one; . . . so that the world may believe that thou (Father) hast sent me" and again, "That they may become perfectly one, so that the world may know that thou hast sent me and hast loved them even as thou hast loved me" (John 17:21, 23). It was God's plan that the Church should be the place where he brought about reconciliation between himself and men and between men and their fellow-men through Christ. This reconciliation of all men with the Father in Christ is a mystery, the inmost essence of which is always concealed from man, but which is nonetheless shown to the world as a truly sensational sign in the reconciliation of man with his fellow-men. God manifests to the world the invisible grace of his reconciliation in the visible brotherhood of Christians. Christian unity — the harmonious life of Christians together in one house in a spirit of mutual goodwill and tolerance, their dwelling together in one mind, caring for each other and especially for those who are weak, ill or poor — this is a light shining before the world. "For it is the God who said, 'Let light shine out of darkness,' who has shone in our hearts to give the light of the knowledge of the glory of God in the face of Christ" (2 Cor. 4:6).

The lack of brotherly love within the Church is a constant shadow on the face of Christ, which the world ought to recognize in the Church, in other words, in our life together as Christians.

The sign of unity is not, however, impaired only by the lack of brotherly love within the Church. It has also lost much of its luster through the many separations and divisions that have taken place throughout the history of Christianity — divisions which have continued up to the present day. Countless temporary dwellings have been erected in the course of time around the house of Peter. This is not the place to talk about guilt — more and more Christians are now becoming convinced that the blame must be shared. But the simple fact remains that, out of every six people in the world, there are only two Christians, and that these Christians are moreover divided among themselves — one of the two lives in the house of Peter and the other in one of the many houses belonging to one or other of the separated Christian groups. And this fact is the scandal of Christianity today. The Gospel, which announces, as its essential message, the universal

brotherhood of all men in Christ under the fatherhood of the one God, is proclaimed in "gospels" that
are mutually contradictory, and by preachers who
refuse fellowship with each other. This implies a
great responsibility for all Christians, both for those
who have left the house of Peter and for those who
remain in it. Among the scandals given by Christians
to the world, the sin of separation is perhaps the
most shameful and humiliating. It is also to be hoped
that it is at the same time the sin which makes the
most powerful claim on our conscious idea of faith.

Love of our brothers is not only a sign for the
world. It is also a sign for those who believe. "By
this we may be sure that we know him, if we keep
his commandments. He who says, 'I know him' but
disobeys his commandments is a liar, and the truth
is not in him; but whoever keeps his word, in him
truly love for God is perfected. By this we may be
sure that we are in him . . . I am writing you no
new commandment, but an old commandment . . .
He who says he is in the light and hates his brother
is in the darkness still. He who loves his brother
abides in the light" (1 John 2:3-10). "By this it may
be seen who are the children of God, and who are
the children of the devil: whoever does not do right
is not of God, nor he who does not love his brother.
For this is the message which you have heard from
the beginning, that we should love one another . . .
We know that we have passed out of death into
life, because we love the brethren. He who does
not love remains in death . . . By this we know love,

that he laid down his life for us; and we ought to
lay down our lives for the brethren" (1 John 3:10-11,
14-16).

Love of his brothers is the decisive distinguishing
mark of the Christian because it is a direct consequence of the mystery of our redemption. This
mystery is nothing other than God himself, who has
created this fellowship between himself and men.
This mystery, which was originally contained in the
invisible God, entered our world through the incarnation of God's Son and has since that time been
experienced in a visible community of men. God's
fatherhood was revealed and given to us in the Son,
who became our fellow-man and made us his and
each others' brothers. Brotherly love is a direct
continuation of God's love. The two are inseparable,
and that is why reconciliation with our brothers is
manifestly a sign of the veracity of our reconciliation
with God. "Beloved, let us love one another; for
love is of God, and he who loves is born of God and
knows God. He who does not love does not know
God; for God is love. In this the love of God was
made manifest among us, that God sent his only
Son into the world, so that we might live through
him. In this is love, not that we loved God but that
he loved us and sent his Son to be the expiation for
our sins. Beloved, if God so loved us, we also ought
to love one another. No man has ever seen God;
if we love one another, God abides in us and his
love is perfected in us. By this we know that we
abide in him and he in us, because he has given us

of his own Spirit . . . If anyone says, 'I love God,' and hates his brother, he is a liar; for he who does not love his brother whom he has seen, cannot love God whom he has not seen. And this commandment we have from him, that he who loves God should love his brother also" (1 John 4:7-13, 20-21).

Brotherly love, then, is a gift from God and at the same time a task given to us by God. Because, and insofar as this love is a gift of God, this brotherly bond will, like the Church herself, never disappear from this world. But, because and insofar as this brotherly unity is a task which has been given to us by God, it will never be able to exist without sacrifices on our part and it will never maintain an unthreatened existence. We are much more aware these days than we have been in the past of the harm that the brotherhood of Christians has suffered because of these historical divisions. These cannot, it is true, be attributed exclusively to a lack of brotherly love, either on the part of those who have left the Catholic Church or on the part of those who have remained in it — according to both, it was first and foremost the handing down of God's Gospel in its pure form that was at stake. Yet the division certainly did not come about only because of conflicting views about the truth of the Gospel. Christian brotherly love suffered grievously during the dispute over the truth, and this happened because Christians had previously been intolerant of each other and unable to listen to each other without prejudice. Mutual antipathy and suspicion prevented a genuine joint consultation at the source of truth. If we want to find ways now towards the reunion of all baptized Christians, we shall have to go through the whole dispute in the reverse order. If we are to achieve this full unity, which is a unity of truth in love, we shall have to begin by loving each other and by experiencing anew the brotherhood which is given to us at baptism. "Speaking the truth in love, we are to grow up in every way into him who is the head, into Christ" (Eph. 4:15).

7

ONE, EVEN AS WE ARE ONE

It was on the eve of his sacrifice on the Cross that the Lord took his disciples more deeply than on any other occasion into the mystery of Christian unity. The Israelites were at this time gathered around the ritual meal of the Passover to commemorate the miraculous birth of their nation and to renew their covenant with the God who had brought them together as his people. While this feast was taking place, Jesus revealed to his own the mystery of the origin of the new people of God and inaugurated the New Covenant.

The news of Jesus' return to the Father had startled the disciples. They feared the dissolution of their association with him, the fellowship which had developed so slowly and upon which they had staked their whole lives. But Jesus showed them the deeper foundations of their togetherness and affirmed that their unity with him and with each other was a direct extension of that supreme and unimaginable unity experienced by God himself. He revealed to them that his departure as a man from the association together with them in this world and his return to the full togetherness with the Father was the creation and the revelation of an imperishable fellowship between the triune God, and those who believed in the Son. Christian unity, which is experienced by us as a terrestrial reality, comes from God as the Trinity — from the Father, the Son and the Holy Spirit, who live together in an intensely reciprocal relationship in the most sublime unity. The mystery of Christian unity has its origin in the first of all Christian mysteries, the life of the three distinct Persons in the one God. Jesus did not "explain" the unity of his disciples, but referred to the mystery of God. This reference was intended to arouse in those who believed in him an awareness which would fill them with an even deeper reverence, to make them see that Christian unity is an object of their faith, and something holy.

Jesus made his disciples conscious of this connection between the mystery of Christian unity and the mystery of God by approaching the subject from various points of view. First of all, he affirmed his personal unity with the Father. Thomas' question about the way to the Father provided him with his opportunity, and he declared that he was himself the way, and that no one came to the Father, but by him. "If you had known me," he went on, "you would have known my Father also; henceforth you know him and have seen him." Philip then asked him, "Lord, show us the Father, and we shall be satisfied." Jesus' reply to this request was: "Have I been with you so long, and yet you do not know me, Philip? He who has seen me has seen the

Father; how can you say, 'Show us the Father?'
Do you not believe that I am in the Father and the
Father in me? The words that I say to you I do not
speak on my own authority; but the Father who
dwells in me does his works. Believe me that I am
in the Father and the Father in me; or else believe
me for the sake of the works themselves" (John
14:7-11). A few moments later, Jesus said again: "The
word which you hear is not mine, but the Father's
who sent me" (John 14:24). These statements can be
compared with what Jesus had previously said, crying
out: "He who believes in me, believes not in me but
in him who sent me. And he who sees me sees him
who sent me" (John 12:44-45). These words formed
the conclusion of the parables of the one Shepherd
and the one flock to which all those who believed in
him and in the works that he did in his Father's
name, which bore witness to him (John 10:25), would
belong, for "I and the Father are one" (John 10:30).

The Father and the Son cannot be separated from
each other. As Jesus says of himself: "I am not alone,
for the Father is with me" (John 16:32). The Father
constantly calls the Son to mind and the Son the
Father. In the one God the first Person cannot be
without the second. Both live the one, full divine
life, and are only distinguished from each other in
that the one, as the Father, is completely orientated
towards the Son, in order thus to be himself, that is,
God, and in that the other, as the Son, is completely
orientated towards the Father, also in order to be
himself, God. The divine Persons are completely

equal. Each experiences the one divine life as his own, but each experiences it at the same time as a constant orientation towards the other. Each of the divine Persons experiences his "ego" in fullness but in a reciprocal relationship. In God is expressed — in a way which is for us completely inaccessible and unimaginable — the most sublime and perfect unity of distinct Persons who are completely merged into each other without losing themselves. They are completely themselves by being entirely turned towards each other.

This sublime unity between the Father and the Son was made visible by the Son's works, which were equally the works of the Father, and by the Son's words, which were equally the words of the Father. This explains why Jesus was able to promise that he would do everything that the disciples asked the Father in his name — "Whatever you ask the Father in my name, he will give it to you" (John 15:16) and "If you ask anything in my name, I will do it" (John 14:14). Similarly Jesus speaks about the Holy Spirit as the one sent by the Father (John 14:16), as the one sent by the Father in his name (John 14:26) and as the one sent by himself (John 16:7).

The third Person in God, the Holy Spirit who proceeds from the Father and the Son, also manifested to the disciples this holy unity in God. Just as the Father and the Son spoke the same words, so was this "other Counsellor," in Jesus' words, to "teach you all things, and bring to your remembrance all that I have said to you" (John 14:26; cf. also 14:16).

"When the Spirit of truth comes, he will guide you
into all the truth; for he will not speak on his own
authority, but whatever he hears he will speak, . . .
he will take what is mine and declare it to you.
All that the Father has is mine; therefore, I said
that he will take what is mine and declare it to you"
(John 16:13-15).

Jesus extended this sublime unity in God to his
community. In the parable of the Shepherd and
the flock, he said: "I know my own and my own
know me, as the Father knows me and I know the
Father" (John 10:14). During the Last Supper, he
said: "As the Father has loved me, so have I loved
you; abide in my love. If you keep my commandments, you will abide in my love, just as I have kept
my Father's commandments and abide in his love"
(John 15:9-10). In his discourse on the Eucharist, he
used the term "life," "to live" (this should be compared with "know" and "love" in the preceding
passages): "As the living Father sent me, and I live
because of the Father, so he who eats me will live
because of me" (John 6:57).

In these passages, the Lord used the construction
"As . . . so . . ." and this is in itself an indication of
a miraculous connection. But Jesus made this association even stronger when he said: "I do not say
to you that I shall pray the Father for you; for the
Father himself loves you, because you have loved
me and have believed that I came from the Father"
(John 16:26-27) and "If a man loves me, he will keep
my word, and my Father will love him, and we will

come to him and make our home with him" (John 14:23).

The expression "to abide in" is one of the most incisive and striking of all the biblical definitions of unity as a lasting and intimate presence with each other. Jesus used it in his unforgettable parable of the true vine: "I am the true vine, and my Father is the vinedresser. Every branch of mine that bears no fruit, he takes away, and every branch that does bear fruit he prunes, that it may bear more fruit. You are already made clean by the word which I have spoken to you. Abide in me, and I in you. As the branch cannot bear fruit by itself, unless it abides in the vine, neither can you, unless you abide in me. I am the vine, you are the branches. He who abides in me, and I in him, he it is that bears much fruit, for apart from me you can do nothing. If a man does not abide in me, he is cast forth as a branch and withers; and the branches are gathered, thrown into the fire and burned. If you abide in me, and my words abide in you, ask whatever you will, and it shall be done for you. By this my Father is glorified, that you bear much fruit, and so prove to be my disciples" (John 15:1-8).

The Lord situated this mutual abiding in each other of himself and his own within the context of the unity in God, and tried to make his disciples understand that "I am in the Father, and you in me, and I in you" (John 14:20). He enlarged on this theme in his prayer for the apostles.[13]

Jesus' prayer on the eve of his death on the Cross

requires little commentary. Although there are fre-
quent references in the gospels to the fact that Jesus
prayed, the content of his prayer is seldom reproduced, and when it is, it usually occupies at the most
one or two verses (Cf. Matt. 11:25; John 11:41-42).
On the last occasion that he was with his own, however, Jesus spoke openly to the Father, so that they
might have his "joy fulfilled in themselves" (John
17:13). No other passage in Scripture shows to such
an extent Jesus' sharing in what filled his heart. His
mind was entirely occupied with his function of
mediation and reconciliation. He prayed that he
might be admitted to the Father, as a sign that his
mediation was accepted, and he prayed too for his
own who were still in the world, that they might be
preserved. This preservation of the disciples was described by Jesus as a "preservation from evil," a "sanc-
tification in the truth of God's word" and a "being
kept together." A single reality is expressed by these
three terms — Jesus prayed that his own should remain together in the Father's love. He asked for
this first of all for the apostles and then "for those
who believe in me through their word."

"He lifted up his eyes to heaven and said, 'Father,
the hour has come; glorify thy Son that the Son may
glorify thee, since thou hast given him power over
all flesh, to give eternal life to all whom thou hast
given him. And this is eternal life, that they know
thee the only true God, and Jesus Christ whom
thou hast sent. I glorified thee on earth, having
accomplished the work which thou gavest me to

do; and now, Father, glorify me in thy own presence with the glory which I had with thee before the world was made.

"I have manifested thy name to the men whom thou gavest me out of the world; thine they were, and thou gavest them to me, and they have kept thy word . . . Holy Father, keep them in thy name, which thou hast given me, that they may be one, even as we are one. While I was with them, I kept them in thy name, which thou hast given me . . . I do not pray that thou shouldst take them out of the world, but that thou shouldst keep them from the evil one. They are not of the world, even as I am not of the world. Sanctify them in the truth; thy word is truth. As thou didst send me into the world, so I have sent them into the world. And for their sake I consecrate myself, that they also may be consecrated in truth.

"I do not pray for these only, but also for those who believe in me through their word, that they may all be one; even as thou, Father, art in me, and I in thee, that they also may be in us, so that the world may believe that thou hast sent me. The glory which thou hast given me I have given to them, that they may be one even as we are one, I in them and thou in me, that they may become perfectly one, so that the world may know that thou hast sent me and hast loved them even as thou hast loved me" (John 17:1-6, 11-12, 15-23).

Toward the end of this prayer, Jesus was entirely concerned with the unity of his own, referring to it three times within the space of a few sentences. These words occur within a context of holy truth and love. Unity, truth and love — all three come from God; they were in the first place bestowed upon the Son, as his glory, and he communicated them to his own. This was later to be manifested as a startling reality, when the Father resurrected his Son from death and made him sit at his right hand — the Son's glory, hitherto concealed, was then to shine forth. Jesus had already told his disciples about that moment: "In that day you will know that I am in my Father, and you in me, and I in you" (John 14:20).

At this time, Jesus was already standing on the threshold of that glory. Its luster had fallen on the table at which he had just celebrated the Eucharist and shared it with his disciples. The mediator was on the point of dedicating himself in a perfect sacrifice to the Father, so that his own, totally dedicated to God, might also be holy. Thus they too would come to share fully in his glory: "Father, I desire that they also, whom thou hast given me, may be with me where I am, to behold my glory which thou hast given me in thy love for me before the foundation of the world" (John 17:24). Even while the disciples were still in the world, however, the luster of this as yet veiled glory was already becoming apparent. The fellowship with God which had been given to them, but which was still not public (1 John 3:2), was already beginning to manifest itself in their experience as God's children and as each others' brothers. "Peace I leave with you; my peace

I give to you; not as the world gives do I give to you" (John 14:27). This unity in joy, which came from God and which had its beginning at the Lord's Supper, was to be a sign to the world of the truth of the Son and of his having been sent by the Father (John 17:21), and a testimony of God's love for his Son and for those who received him (5:23).

Jesus made his most profound revelation of the mystery of Christian unity not in the form of an in-struction, but in a prayer, thus showing us quite clearly that the unity of the Church could never be our achievement. Both the creation and the preser-vation of this unity are a lasting gift of God. We, who have to be constantly "preserved in unity" (cf. John 17:11), have therefore to pray without ceasing for this gift. We human beings are, by birth and origin, scattered and divided. Each one of us is turned towards himself. God's grace alone can take us out of this individual isolation and bring us to-gether in fellowship. Yet, whenever we have in fact received the grace of unity with God and with each other, and especially when we see this grace in a visible form in the world, we are at once susceptible to the temptation to regard this unity as a result of our own labors, and to pride ourselves on having built this "citadel of unity," forgetting that "Unless the Lord builds the house, those who build it labor in vain" (Ps. 127:1). In this respect, the unity of the Church is a gift requiring very delicate handling. The slightest feeling of self-satisfaction on the part of those who receive it, either individually or col-

lectively, casts a shadow over it. There is indeed
some truth in the suggestion that God has permitted
the divisions that have occurred throughout the
course of time so that men should not forget that
unity is a grace. It cannot be denied that there is
a distressing and anguished note in the Lord's thrice
repeated prayer "that they may be one." Jesus
knew the future history of his Church. Throughout
the whole of her existence, from the earliest days
until the present time, the Church's unity in truth
and love has been accompanied by discord. The
earliest liturgical prayer known to us contains a plea
for unity: "Be mindful, O Lord, of thy Church, and
free her from all evil; perfect her in thy love and
gather her, thy sanctified one, from the four quarters
of the earth into thy Kingdom" (Didache, chapter
10). The Church has always been compelled to pray
in this way, especially during the celebration of
the eucharistic sacrament of unity. The Church is
praying for unity today with an even deeper sense
of guilt and of needing help and with the ever-
increasing consent of a growing number of her
faithful. This is the work of the Spirit of the Church,
who is already causing the shadow of the many
divisions in Christianity to recede. And the Holy
Spirit would not make us ask so urgently for this
grace if he had not already begun to give us what
we are praying for.

Finally, it should be remembered that the Lord
said this prayer as our high priest, standing before
the Holy of Holies to make sacrifice. He had al-

ready made his giving away of himself present to the apostles under the signs of bread and wine, and was on the point of bringing the new community into the world in his sacrifice on the Cross. We, who were once far from God and from each other, were made one by his blood and reconciled to God through his Cross (Cf. Eph. 2:13-16). The community of the Church was born on the Cross and will bear the sacrifice of the Cross as one of her marks throughout all generations. Sacrifices will always be demanded of all the faithful, as part of their living and remaining together in the one Church of Christ. They will be called upon to make sacrifices of the spirit and of the heart, of their talents and of their material possessions. It may not always be simply a question of abandoning error and sin, but even a **kenosis,** like Christ's emptying of himself (cf. Phil. 2:7), with regard to things which in themselves are permitted. The apostle's praise of those who abstain from what is permitted so that their brothers may not be needlessly scandalized (cf. Rom. 14:1-23) can certainly be applied to such Christians today, at a time of necessary renewal of Christian unity and of making this unity accessible to all baptized Christians. Even St. Paul's statement about the eating of unclean flesh from the pagan temples is applicable to Christians today. If we realize that there are no false gods, then "food will not commend us to God. We are no worse off if we do not eat (unclean flesh), and no better off if we do. Only we must take care lest this liberty of ours somehow become a stumbling block to the weak. For if any one sees me, a man of knowledge, at table in an idol's temple, might he not be encouraged, if his conscience is weak, to eat food offered to idols? And so by my knowledge this weak man is destroyed, the brother for whom Christ died. Thus, sinning against our brethren and wounding their consciences when they are weak, we sin against Christ. Therefore, if food is a cause of my brother's falling, I will never eat meat, lest I cause my brother to fall" (1 Cor. 8:8-13).

8

OF ONE HEART AND SOUL

The history of Christ's Church began with a period of remarkable singleness of mind. This was the time — the first ten years following the ascension of the Lord — during which the whole Church was centered in Jerusalem.

Immediately after the Lord's return to his Father, the apostles were together with a group of faithful followers and "all these with one accord devoted themselves to prayer" (Acts 1:14). The first matter to be settled by general consent of all present was the choice of a successor to Judas. Peter, raising this question, "stood up among the brethren and said, 'Brethren . . .'" (Acts 1:15-16). Those who previously had been called "disciples" were now known by the characteristic name of "brethren," a word which occurs about a hundred and sixty times with this meaning in the Acts of the Apostles and the epistles, and even in the phrase "false brethren" (Gal. 2:4). Its meaning was not derived from family, racial, national or historical relationships, but exclusively from Christ, who made all those who did his Father's will his brothers and called them by this name (Cf. chapter II, p. 32 ff, on the idea of Christian brotherhood).

The band of brothers was open to receive new members when the Spirit of Christ descended on them on the day of Pentecost and "they were all together in one place" (Acts 2:1). The little community now appeared in the forum of the world as the ecumenical Church, as the community created for the purpose of bringing the whole of the **oikoumene,** that is, all the inhabited world, into unity with and in Christ and thus to become itself a Christian **oikoumene** in which all would live together as brothers around the First-born under the universal fatherhood of the one God. The Spirit manifested the dynamic ecumenism of the one community of Christ in "a rush of mighty wind" which "filled all the house where they were sitting," in "tongues of fire" and in prompting all those who were present to bear witness in many languages. Cutting across the linguistic and cultural limitations of the twelve Galileans, the Spirit gathered "Parthians and Medes and Elamites and residents of Mesopotamia, Judea and Cappadocia, Pontus and Asia, Phrygia and Pamphylia, Egypt and the parts of Libya belonging to Cyrene and visitors from Rome, both Jews and proselytes, Cretans and Arabians" around "Peter, standing with the eleven" (Acts 2:1-11, 14). This astonishing event and Peter's testimony and proclamation caused "about three thousand souls" to join the Church. According to the graphic Greek and Latin texts, these people were "added" to the apostolic community (Cf. Acts 2:41).

The first reception into Christian unity followed

a procedure, the individual moments of which were to characterize all such receptions throughout all time. Firstly, the apostles preached Christ. They spoke about his divine mission, his life among men, his death and his return to the Father, when he was made the "Lord" of all who were to be saved. Then those who were moved by the apostles' testimony of Christ asked the Church: "What shall we do?" The answer was: "Repent, and be baptized." Conversion, or repentance, meant a readiness to submit all thought, action and will to the decisive saving fact of Christ's appearance and universal mediation, since joining him involved the acceptance of a "doctrine of life" (Acts 5:20). Being baptized was on the one hand an essential confession of faith in Jesus Christ (Cf. Acts 8:16; 10:48; 19:5; 22:6; cf. also Rom. 6:3; Gal. 3:27; 1 Cor. 1:13, 16; 6:11; 10:2). On the other hand, it was prayer for absolute forgiveness of sins. When the Church administers baptism, she accepts this confession of faith and mediates in the forgiveness of sins given by Christ together with the gift of his Holy Spirit (Cf. Acts 2:38; 5:32; 9:17-18). That these words and actions also really accomplish what they aim to convey was affirmed by God on several occasions during these early years by the sensually perceptible phenomena which accompanied the descent of the Holy Spirit (Cf. Acts 8:14-19; 10:44; 19:1-6).

The inner unity of faith and love was manifested in four characteristics: "They devoted themselves to the apostles' teaching and fellowship, to the breaking of bread and the prayers" (Acts 2:42). These four marks were to characterize for all time the unity of the Church — one single confession of faith on a basis of apostolic testimony, a life together in harmony based on the many-sided dialogue of full human relationships, the celebration of the Eucharist as the sign of the grace of the New Covenant and finally communal prayer as a glorification "with one voice glorify the God and Father of our Lord Jesus Christ" (Rom. 15:6; cf. also Eph. 5:19-20).

In the beginning, while they were still "together in one place" and the community was still relatively small, the living together of Christians in harmony was particularly stressed: "All who believed were together and had all things in common; and they sold their possessions and goods and distributed them to all, as any had need. And day by day, attending the temple and breaking bread in their homes, they partook of food with glad and generous hearts" (Acts 2:44-46). Even when the Christian community had grown until "the number of the men came to about five thousand" (Acts 4:4), Luke was able to testify: "The company of those who believed were of one heart and soul, and no one said that any of the things which he possessed was his own, but they had everything in common" and "there was not a needy person among them, for as many as were possessors of lands or houses sold them, and brought the proceeds of what was sold and laid it at the apostles' feet; and distribution was made to each as any had need" (Acts 4:32, 34-35). This communal way of life was naturally very difficult to maintain in the fast-growing community of Jerusalem and impossible to preserve when the faithful had become dispersed among different communities.

Yet the Church has never been able to forget her beginning as one single mother community. Again and again throughout her history, men have taken the initiative in an attempt to revive this way of life in smaller groups. This way of life in perfect fellowship, sharing the Eucharist, prayers and all possessions, was, as late as the twelfth century, still characterized as the "apostolic way of life." This strict community life, the life of the religious "orders," always comes about especially whenever the Church as a whole is called upon to suffer in her holy truth, love or unity. Viewed in this light then, it is an extremely hopeful sign that communities have arisen in our own times, both inside the Catholic Church and outside, which are committed, in the dedication of their way of life, to the reunion of all Christians.

When, however, the young Church became dispersed over various places, there arose a practice, in accordance with the spirit of the original sharing of all possessions, which entailed the making of collections from various communities for the support of others in need of help. Unity thus continued to be experienced among the brothers living in different places by "generosity of contribution" (2 Cor. 9:13). This idea was already familiar to the Jews. So that the thought that they formed one single nation might be kept alive in the minds of all Jews dispersed throughout the world, a tax had been imposed on all men above the age of twenty for the upkeep of the temple, the central point for the whole of Israel. St. Paul probably took over this idea from the Jews, but he laid particular stress on the voluntary nature of the contributions (Cf. 2 Cor. 8:3, 8-17; 9:7). The apostle repeatedly emphasized the importance of these collections in order to strengthen the bond between the mother community in Jerusalem, which consisted predominantly of Christians of Jewish origin, and the other communities, whose members were in the main Christians of gentile origin (Cf. Acts 11:29-30; 24:17; Rom. 15:25-31; 1 Cor. 16:1-4; 2 Cor. 8:1-14; 9: Gal. 3:10). These "gifts of love" (1 Cor. 16:3) were not simply expressions of a readiness to help. They gave expression to the more profound unity between the Jewish and the gentile Christians, a unity which was later to be threatened by both natural and religious opposition — "If the Gentiles have come to share in their (the Jewish Christians' in Jerusalem) spiritual blessings, they ought also to be of service to them in material blessings" (Rom. 15:27).[14]

The Church's first days were seemingly idyllic — she was still living in the octave of the first Pentecost. But quite early in St. Luke's account there is an indication that the holy unity of the Church was threatened. The married couple, Ananias and Sapphira, sold some of their property and laid a part of the proceeds at the apostles' feet, in the pretense that they were giving the whole of their possessions to the community. Peter condemned what they had done as a "deception of the Holy Spirit," as "lying not to men but to God" and as a "temptation of the Spirit of the Lord" (Acts 5:1-10). When they had heard these words, both Ananias and his wife died. Their sin, which incurred so terrible a punishment, was not in the first place their pretense, or even their retention as such of some of the money, since there was no obligation to contribute to the Church (Cf. Acts 5:4). The sin, punished by God himself in this awe-inspiring way by sudden death, was the violation of the sacred unity of the Christian community and the desecration of the holy people of God — the contempt of the divine element that was so clearly visible in the new community. The death of Ananias and Sapphira calls to mind the death of the man Uzzah, who rashly put out his hand to the holy ark in which God himself dwelt among his people while it was being taken to Jerusalem (Cf. 2 Sam. 6:9). The reaction of those around was the same in both cases — they were filled with awe (Acts 5:11; 2 Sam. 6:9). The sentence, pronounced by Peter and carried out by God, was an impressive sign of the presence of the Holy One himself in his community — his dwelling among them as in his sacred ark.

It was not long before the communal sharing of all possessions led to a new threat to Christian unity. Their harmonious state of being "all together in Solomon's Portico" (Acts 5:12) was disrupted by a quarrel between the Palestinian Jewish Christians, the Hebrews, and the hellenized Jewish Christians from the Diaspora. These hellenized Jews, who differed from the Palestinian Jews in language and culture, were quite numerous in Jerusalem and even had their own synagogue (Acts 6:9). It is also probable that hellenistic Jews from outside Jerusalem had joined the Christian community when they had been struck by the miracle of Pentecost during their pilgrimage to the City at the time of the great Jewish feasts. These Jews would have been especially dependent upon the help and hospitality of the baptized Hebrews. In any case, the question of the support of widows caused a great deal of friction between the two groups of Christianized Jews — the hellenistic Jews felt themselves to have been passed over in favor of the Hebrews. The conflict assumed serious proportions and the apostles summoned the whole community to discuss it. On the suggestion of the apostles, seven candidates were selected by the community for appointment as deacons with pastoral duties and the apostles prayed and laid their hands upon these men, thus conferring upon them the power to discharge their office. What is remarkable is that, as soon as the single-minded unity of the community had been restored, both the authority of the apostles and the willing cooperation of the whole community made themselves powerfully felt again (Acts 6:1-6). This experience within the community may well have contributed to the result described by Luke in the following verse: "And the word of God increased; and the number

of the disciples multiplied greatly in Jerusalem"
(Acts 6:7).

After some years, however, the community in Jerusalem became involved in a long period of crisis.
The cause of this crisis was the spread of the Church
outside the walls of the City — this had in fact been
set in motion by the persecution of the faithful by
the Council of the Jews. The breach between ancient
Israel and the new Israel had come into the open.
Until then, the apostolic community, known as the
Nazarenes (Acts 24:5) had been tolerated in Israel.
Its members were, after all, still Jews who went to
the temple, and the formation of groups for religious
reasons was a familiar occurrence in Israel. The
Council of the Jews, which had from the very beginning viewed the Christian community with dis-
favor, had arrested Peter and John (Acts 4:1-23)
and shortly afterwards all the apostles (Acts 5:17-41).
But, because the people were very favorably disposed
towards the new community (Acts 2:47; 4:21; 5:13),
the Council had been unable to intervene decisively.
The enthusiastic appearance of the deacon Stephen,
however, presented the Council with the opportunity
for which it had been waiting, and Stephen was
accused of speaking against the temple and the Mosaic law (Acts 6:8-15; 7:1-53). Stephen blamed the
Council openly for being unfaithful to the promise
given by God to Israel and to the Law and for
murdering Jesus. This resulted in the death of
Stephen and the violent persecution of the Church
in Jerusalem (Acts 7:54-59; 8:1).

The faithful fled from Jerusalem. Many were
scattered throughout Judea, Galilee and Samaria and
many of the Hellenists returned to the coastal region
of Phoenicia, to Cyprus and to Antioch, the third
capital of the Roman Empire. In this way, the per-
secuted Church fulfilled the words of the Lord:
"You shall be my witnesses in Jerusalem and in all
Judea and Samaria and to the end of the earth"
(Acts 1:8). She gave form to her call to be universal,
since "those who were scattered went about preaching
the word" (Acts 8:4). Their preaching was heard
with faith, first of all in Palestine, and it was not
long before the apostles were laying their hands upon
the newly baptized Christians and praying for them
to receive the Holy Spirit (Acts 8:14-17). When the
persecution had burnt itself out, the Church had
members in "all Judea and Galilee and Samaria . . .
and in the comfort of the Holy Spirit it was multiplied" and Peter travelled around visiting the scattered communities (Acts 9:31-32).

It was on one of these journeys that Peter was
urged by the Lord himself to receive the first gentiles into the Church (Acts 10). The baptism of Cor-
nelius and his family, household and friends made
Peter aware of the universal nature of the Christian
faith, an idea which he communicated to his amazed
brethren immediately on his return to Jerusalem:
"Truly I perceive that God shows no partiality, but
in every nation any one who fears him and does
what is right is acceptable to him. You know the
word which he sent to Israel, preaching good news

of peace by Jesus Christ: he is Lord of all" (Acts 10:34-36; cf. also 1 Pet. 1:17). Peter's convincing testimony, moreover, made the community begin to realize that "to the Gentiles also God has granted repentance unto life" (Acts 11:18).

This marked the entry of the Church into a new phase of life, the beginning of her fulfillment of the permanent function for which she was intended, that is, to be the one house for all peoples. The young Church needed time to grow towards this destiny, and the apostolic epistles had to come back again and again to the fact that there was "no distinction between Jew and Greek," that there was "neither slave nor free, neither male nor female," no "circumcised and uncircumcised, barbarian, Scythian," "for you are all one in Christ Jesus," who was "the same Lord of all" and "all in all" (Rom. 10:12; Gal. 3:28; 1 Cor. 12:13; Col. 3:11). This period of growth was not without difficulties for the young community, which had to strip the Jewish Christian form of its unity of those specifically Jewish elements which were not essential to its unity and which were not compatible with its universal nature.

The process of making the Church habitable for all nations was set in motion by the hellenized Jews who, returning from Jerusalem to the Diaspora, successfully established contact with the gentiles: "The hand of the Lord was with them, and a great number that believed turned to the Lord" (Acts 11:21). This was especially so in Antioch, which saw the rapid formation of a community that attracted attention in Jerusalem. The mother community dispatched Barnabas, who was himself a native of Cyprus (Acts 4:36), to sound the feelings and views of the new community. Seeing the "grace of God" in Antioch, Barnabas brought Saul from Tarsus and worked with him in the fast-growing community, which soon became a "large company" (Acts 11:19-26). It was in Antioch that the faithful were first called by the name of "Christians." From this time onward, this was always to be the distinctive name of the members of the new Israel.

Just as the apostles preserved a comprehensive view of the scattered communities in Palestine from Jerusalem, so the mother community also maintained communications with the community in Antioch. Prophets — those among the faithful with the spiritual gift of prophecy — travelled from Jerusalem to Antioch and appeared there, while the Christians of Antioch collected gifts for those who were in distress in Jerusalem (Acts 11:27-30). Paul and Barnabas handed their gifts over to the faithful in the City. Before leaving for Syria and Cilicia, Paul had already gone to Jerusalem "to visit Cephas" (Gal. 1:18). When a conflict arose in Antioch, the community again turned to Jerusalem. The cause of this dissension was the demand made by some of the faithful who had come from Judea that all Christians were bound to be circumcised according to the requirements of the Jews. The result was "no small dissension and debate" (Acts 15:2). The Antiochian community decided to send Paul, Barnabas and a

few companions to the apostles and elders in Jerusalem. This was a critical moment in the develop-
ment of Christ's Church from ancient Israel — her
unity and her universal nature were in the balance.
Paul, the "apostle of the gentiles" (Gal. 2:7-8), was
particularly well aware of the seriousness of the
situation. Wondering whether he had not somehow
"run in vain," he hastened to lay before those who
were men of repute the gospel which he preached
among the gentiles (Cf. Gal. 2:1-2).

In Jerusalem, the apostles, the elders and the
Antiochian envoys took part in frank discussion,
but were unable to reach agreement (Cf. Acts
15:7). Peter then made his historic decision known:
"God who knows the heart bore witness to them,
giving them the Holy Spirit just as he did to us; and
he made no distinction between us and them, but
cleansed their hearts by faith. . . . But we believe
that we shall be saved through the grace of the Lord
Jesus, just as they will" (Acts 15:7-11). The assembly
agreed with this decision. Paul, writing about this
later in his epistle to the Galatians, said: "Titus, who
was with me, was not compelled to be circumcised,
though he was a Greek" (Gal. 2:3).

The Jewish Christians thus sacrificed their own
ideals and their own particular preferences for the
sake of Christian unity. But, in the very same Council, a sacrifice was also demanded of the gentile
Christians. James proposed that the converts from
the gentile world, at least those who were living
together in communities which contained many

Jewish brethren, should observe certain points to which the Jewish Christians, in view of their own tradition, attached importance. According to James, these gentiles should abstain from certain foods and from marriages which came within the various categories of relationship forbidden by Jewish law (Acts 15:13-21). The gentile Christians were ready to accept this rule of conduct, and the assembly was thus in a position to compose a letter as brethren "to the brethren who are of the Gentiles in Antioch and Syria and Cilicia, greeting" (Acts 15:23). Both decisions were introduced in the letter by the significant declaration: "It has seemed good to the Holy Spirit and to us. . . " (5:28). It was the Holy Spirit who enabled the assembly to reach an understanding and who was responsible for the apostolic decision. When the Council broke up, "there were no victors and no vanquished, only reconciled Christians" (Von Lefort).

This first Council of the Church may be taken as a symbol of the ecumenical Church, the dwelling place of so many different people, who nonetheless, whenever they are threatened with estrangement from each other, come together around the apostolic office, in the belief that, through his Spirit, Christ is in their midst. The first Pentecost, which marked the beginning of the Church, was thus experienced once more at the end of the first period in the Church's history. The Judaizers continued to cause unrest until the year 200 or thereabouts, despite St. Paul's statements of Christian principles

in his epistles to the Galatians and the Romans between the years 53 and 58, with the result that the
Church was frequently in need of the renewed grace
of Pentecost. But the gentile converts to Christianity
also had to be admonished: "If you do boast, remember it is not you that support the root, but the
root that supports you. . . . So do not become proud,
but stand in awe" (Rom. 11:18-20). The structure
of society remained unchanged — work was still
divided and as a consequence there was still a distinction between master and servant; but the Christian master had to recognize that his slave was his
brother (Philem. 16), and Christian slaves had to give
their masters even better service because they were
brothers (1 Tim. 6:2). It is surprising how often the
New Testament tells us that God does not discrimi-
nate between persons — he "shows no partiality"
(Acts 10:34; Rom. 2:11; Gal. 2:6; Eph. 6:9; Col. 3:25;
1 Pet. 1:17; James 2:1-5). All Christians are "holy
brethren, who share in a heavenly call" (Heb. 3:1)
and every individual must feel as if he is a member
of "the household of faith" (Gal. 6:10). Inside this
house, we must not be angry with our brothers (cf.
Matt. 5:21-22) or work ourselves up into a passion
about the "speck that is in our brother's eye" (Matt.
7:3) while ignoring our own shortcoming.

With regard to those who are not of the household
of faith, the New Testament advises us to render
an account to everyone who "calls us to account for
the hope that is in us," but to do this "with gentle-
ness and reverence" and with a "clear conscience"

(1 Pet. 3:15-16). The counsels of the earliest period of the Christian community, which still contained echoes of the descent of the Holy Spirit, have always accompanied the Church both as advice and as promises. Baptized Christians are estranged from each other today, and many are looking for ways of coming together. Above all, we must hope for a new Pentecost, when the Spirit, whom "God has sent . . . into our hearts" (Gal. 4:6) will once again make us "of one heart and soul."

9

ONE BODY AND ONE BREAD

The threat of disunity compelled the apostles, and especially St. Paul, to express their awareness of the sacred unity of the Church in forceful and moving language. The epistles of the New Testament contain many examples of such incisive formulations.

The Christian brotherhood, from the very beginning, suffered from human sinfulness in the form of "quarrelling and jealousy" (Rom. 13:13), "selfishness and conceit" (Phil. 2:3), "bitter jealousy and selfish ambition," "wars" and "fightings" and the "speaking of evil" (James 3:13-18; 4:1, 11). From the very earliest days of the Church, there were men who were "lovers of self, lovers of money, proud, arrogant, abusive, disobedient to their parents, ungrateful, . . . holding the form of religion but denying the power of it" (2 Tim. 3:2-5).

The teachers of heresy and false doctrine, however, constituted an even more serious threat to Christian unity — "those who create dissensions and difficulties, in opposition to the doctrine which you have been taught," those who "by fair and flattering words deceive the hearts of the simple-minded" (Rom. 16:17-18), men who indulged in "godless chatter" and "who have swerved from the truth" and "upset the faith" of others (2 Tim. 2:16-18), "false teachers, who will secretly bring in destructive heresies, even denying the Master who bought them" (2 Pet. 2:1), "deceivers, . . . who will not acknowledge the coming of Jesus Christ in the flesh" (2 John 7-9), "ungodly persons" — those who had "secretly gained admission" — who "deny our only Master and Lord, Jesus Christ" and who "set up divisions, worldly people, devoid of the Spirit" (Jude 4,8-16, 19).

The greatest danger which threatened the unity of the various Christian communities in those days, however, came from the so-called Judaizers, against whom St. Paul especially made a determined stand. These men, for the most part Christians of Jewish origin, attempted to impose circumcision and the observation of the Jewish law on the gentile Christians. Claiming that baptism and faith in Christ would otherwise be of no avail, they went about preaching with great zeal that "unless you are circumcised according to the custom of Moses, you cannot be saved" (Acts 15:1). Some gentile Christians, influenced by the teaching of the Judaizers, allowed themselves to be circumcised. Others, however, resisted their teaching. The result was that whole Christian communities were thrown into serious confusion. Many of the gentile Christians appealed to St. Paul, who had taught them that they would be saved through faith in Christ. The Judaizers tried to alienate recent converts from St. Paul by causing them to doubt his apostolic office (Gal.

4:17) and by calling themselves "apostles of Christ" and "superlative apostles" (2 Cor. 11:5, 13; 12:11). According to their interpretation of God's plan, salvation came from the Jews and it was not sufficient for the gentiles merely to believe in the Messiah who had been born of the Jews. Before they could be saved, they too had to become Jews themselves and join the "only Israel" by being circumcised and by keeping the Mosaic law.

This important difference of opinion was the subject discussed at the Council of Jerusalem, and the Judaizers were shown to be in the wrong. Both Jews and gentiles were saved by the grace of Jesus Christ, and the Jewish yoke was not to be placed on the necks of the gentiles (Acts 15:8-11). There were, however, still some Judaizers who wanted to make their view prevail and, in order to do so, they appealed to the unique position occupied by the people of Israel since Abraham. They found it impossible to forget — or perhaps it would be more true to say that they did not know how to interpret in the new situation — what had been said so many times under the Old Covenant, that there was but one Yahweh and one Israel, and that these were intimately bound to each other in eternal faithfulness (Cf., for example, Deut. 5:4).

St. Paul allayed the threat of division by a double argument. The holiness of Israel, her being set apart by God's promise, circumcision and the law — all these were indeed a fact, but circumcision and the law gave way now that God's promise had been fulfilled in the coming of Christ (Cf. Rom. 2:1-4, 25; 9:1-11; Gal. 2:1-5, 12). Israel's unique position as a closed unity confronted by the multiplicity of the gentile peoples had passed over into a new phase of God's saving plan, in which he had brought both the faithful Jews and the believing gentiles together into one new people, the new Israel. Yahweh had not forsaken Israel, he had fulfilled his promise and had, in so doing, transferred the faithful Jews in Christ to a new phase in which both they and the believers from the gentile world were included in the one eternal people of God.

The principle of unity of the renewed people of God was Jesus Christ who, as the second Adam, was the ancestor of the new community. His appearance meant the fulfillment of a long period of preparation, the expiry of the laws which isolated Israel as a nation from other nations and the end of the earlier differences between Jew and gentile. "The law was our custodian until Christ came, that we might be justified by faith. But now that faith has come, we are no longer under a custodian; for in Christ Jesus you are all sons of God, through faith. For as many of you as were baptized into Christ have put on Christ. There is neither Jew nor Greek, . . . for you are all one in Christ Jesus" (Gal. 3:24-29). "A man is justified by faith apart from the works of law. Or is God the God of Jews only? Is he not the God of Gentiles also? Yes, of Gentiles also, since God is one; and he will justify the circumcised on the ground of their faith and the uncircumcised through their faith" (Rom. 3:28-30). Since Christ's appearance, then, both believing gentiles and believing Jews became "sons of Abraham" (Gal. 3:7; cf. also 3:9, 29; Rom. 4:16; 9:7).

God recreated Israel, making her a new people in Christ, and he accomplished in the case of the gentiles what he had promised through the prophecy of Hosea: "Those who were not my people I will call 'my people,' and her who was not my beloved I will call 'my beloved.' And in the very place where it was said to them, 'You are not my people,' they will be called 'sons of the living God'" (Hos. 2:23; 1:10; Rom. 9:25-26). There was, in this renewed people, "no distinction between Jew and Greek" and "the same Lord" was "Lord of all" (Rom. 10:12). The gentiles who, before the coming of Christ, were "alienated from the commonwealth of Israel" and as such "strangers and sojourners" became "fellow citizens with the saints and members of the household of God" as soon as Christ had led Israel into the definitive stage of her existence (Eph. 2:12, 19).

In his description of this new unity, St. Paul made use of striking images, both to impress upon Jewish and gentile Christians their profound unity in Christ and to present them with compelling reasons for complete singleness of mind.

The Man Jesus Christ gave us salvation and he is the only savior. Coming to salvation means that we are made one with him — we are incorporated, or better, embodied into him. Under the New Covenant, the people of God became the "Body of

Christ," the salvation of the many became a life
in the one Christ and the many themselves were
clothed with Christ. Addressing his words to the
gentile Christians, Paul wrote not only about the
fact that they formed one single people with the
baptized Jews, but also about the fact that both
groups had been "created one new man" by Christ:
"But now in Christ Jesus you who were once far
off have been brought near in the blood of Christ.
For he is our peace, who has made us both one, and
has broken down the dividing wall of hostility, by
abolishing in his flesh the law of commandments and
ordinances, that he might create in himself one new
man in place of the two, so making peace, and
might reconcile us both to God in one body" (Eph.
2:13-16). Summing up all the elements which made
for unity in a single short passage in the same epistle,
St. Paul said: "There is one body and one Spirit,
just as you were called to the one hope that belongs
to your call, one Lord, one faith, one baptism, one
God and Father of us all, who is above all and
through all and in all" (Eph. 4:4-6).

St. Paul used the image of the Christian community as one body at various levels. In the first
place, he referred to the human body as an organism
in which the members, though different from each
other, form a unity and are only able to function
within that unity, while achieving the aim of the
whole by their mutual diversity. "For as in one
body we have many members and all the members
do not have the same function, so we, though many,

are one body in Christ, and individually members
one of another. Having gifts that differ according
to the grace given to us, let us use them: if prophecy,
in proportion to our faith; if service, in our serving;
he who teaches, in his teaching; he who exhorts, in
his exhortation; he who contributes, in liberality;
he who gives aid, with zeal; he who does acts of
mercy, with cheerfulness" (Rom. 12:4-8).

Elsewhere, he elaborated the comparison still
further: "For the body does not consist of one member but of many. If the foot should say, 'Because
I am not a hand, I do not belong to the body,' that
would not make it any less a part of the body. And
if the ear should say, 'Because I am not an eye, I
do not belong to the body,' that would not make
it any less a part of the body. If the whole body
were an eye, where would be the hearing? If the
whole body were an ear, where would be the sense
of smell? But as it is, God arranged the organs,
each one of them, as he chose. If all were a single
organ, where would the body be? As it is, there
are many parts, yet one body. The eye cannot say
to the hand, 'I have no need of you,' nor again the
head to the feet, 'I have no need of you.' On the
contrary, the parts of the body which seem to be
the weaker are indispensable, and those parts of the
body which we think less honorable we invest with
the greater honor, and our unpresentable parts are
treated with greater modesty, which our more pre-
sentable parts do not require. But God has so ad-
justed the body, giving the greater honor to the

inferior part, that there may be no discord in the
body, but that the members may have the same care
for one another. If one member suffers, all suffer
together; if one member is honored, all rejoice together. Now you are the body of Christ and individually members of it. And God has appointed in the
church first the apostles, second prophets, third
teachers, then workers of miracles, then healers,
helpers, administrators, speakers in various kinds of
tongues" (1 Cor. 12:14-28).

Up to this point, Paul's comparison could also be
applied to communities other than that of the Church.
But, by tracing the distinctive unity of the Church
as a body back to the one who inspires this community, he raised it to a higher level. It was the one
Spirit who, according to the apostle, gave life to
the various members of the body, and indeed gave it
life together. "For just as the body is one and has
many members, and all the members of the body,
though many, are one body, so it is with Christ. For
by one Spirit we were all baptized into one body —
Jews or Greeks, slaves or free — and all were made
to drink of one Spirit (1 Cor. 12:12-13). "Now there
are varieties of gifts, but the same Spirit; . . . to one
is given through the Spirit the utterance of wisdom,
and to another the utterance of knowledge according
to the same Spirit, to another faith by the same
Spirit, to another gifts of healing by the one Spirit,
to another the working of miracles, to another prophecy, to another the ability to distinguish between
spirits, to another various kinds of tongues, to another

the interpretation of tongues. All these are inspired by one and the same Spirit, who apportions to each one individually as he wills" (1 Cor. 12:4, 8-11).

It was, then, in St. Paul's view, the inspiration of the Holy Spirit that made the body of the Church "the body of Christ" (1 Cor. 12:27), that made the members "one body in Christ" (Rom. 12:5) or quite simply "Christ" (1 Cor. 12:12). It was one and the same Spirit, who dwelt in Jesus Christ and in the individual believers and who kept them together in one life, just as the human soul inspires all the members of a human body and gives it life as one human being.

The Holy Spirit descended first of all upon the Man Jesus Christ to fill his humanity with divinity as the Son of God. The same Holy Spirit was then sent down upon the faithful (John 7:37-39), and this "Spirit of Christ" continues to arouse in us the same mind and disposition that was in Christ Jesus (Cf. Phil. 2:5). We too have become, according to our measure, children of God. "And because you are sons, God has sent the Spirit of his Son into our hearts, crying, 'Abba! Father!'" (Gal. 4:6). Now God is invoked as Father both by Jesus and by the faithful as with one voice. In this way, we are "conformed to the image of his Son, in order that he might be the first-born among many brethren" (Rom. 8:29). We are "temples of the Holy Spirit." We are not our own, but the Lord's. As "one spirit with him," we are "members of Christ" (Cf. 1 Cor. 6:13-19). We receive this Holy Spirit in baptism and

are thus incorporated into Christ (Cf. 1 Cor. 1:10-17).
We have all been "baptized into one body" because
we have all been "made to drink of one Spirit" (1
Cor. 12:13).

A third aspect of Paul's image of the Church as
a body, in which he shows that Christ himself occupies a special place within that body, insists even
more on the inner relationship between Christ and
his own. Christ is "the head of the body, the church"
(Col. 1:18). It is through him that "the whole body,
joined and knit together by every joint with which
it is supplied, when each part is working properly,
makes bodily growth and upbuilds itself in love"
(Eph. 4:16). As the Head of the body, Christ gives
spiritual vitality, power and movement to every
member, so that his body becomes "the fullness of
him who fills all in all" (Eph. 1:23). "For in him the
whole fullness of deity dwells bodily, and you have
come to fullness of life in him, who is the head"
(Col. 2:9-10). If we wish to live as the sons of God,
we must hold fast to the Head, "from whom the
whole body, nourished and knit together through its
joints and ligaments, grows with a growth that is
from God" (Col. 2:19).

We are thus "called in the one body" (Col. 3:15)
and, by virtue of the indwelling Spirit, form one
body with Christ, who is our Head. But this image
does not simply express the intimate and vital bond
joining the faithful members to Christ and to each
other. It also reflects the deep and tender feelings
which Christ has for us, comparable to the love

that a man has for himself in his own body. "For
no man ever hates his own flesh, but nourishes and
cherishes it, as Christ does the church, because we
are members of his body" (Eph. 5:29-30). This is
why the suffering of his Church also affects the
Lord himself. One of the earliest examples of this
occurred when Paul, as a zealous Jew, was still
persecuting the Christians. The Lord appeared to
him and said: "Saul, Saul, why do you persecute me?"
Paul's reply was to ask him who he was — "Who are
you, Lord?" Jesus answered: "I am Jesus, whom you
are persecuting" (Acts 9:4-5).

As a group, Christians are filled with Christ's
Spirit and with the gifts of that Spirit, just as Christ
is filled with God. The Church is the spiritual sphere
of power in which the incarnate Word lives out his
love for the Father and for men, as in his body. Just
as there is one God, one Word and one Spirit, so
too is the body of Christ one. This intimate relationship of everything in the only begotten Son is brought
about by the one faith and the one love that is preserved in the hearts of those who receive it and is
given a perceptible form in the preaching of the one
gospel, the living together in harmony with the
apostles, prophets, evangelists, pastors and teachers,
the confession of the one baptism and the glorification "together with one voice" of "the God and
Father of our Lord Jesus Christ" (Rom. 15:6; cf.
also Eph. 5:19-20; Col. 3:16).

Christianity is only possible when all Christians
are together. "Welcome one another, therefore, as

Christ has welcomed you" (Rom. 15:7). As a result, "none of us lives to himself, and none of us dies to himself. If we live, we live to the Lord, and if we die, we die to the Lord; so then, whether we live or whether we die, we are the Lord's. For to this end Christ died and lived again, that he might be Lord both of the dead and of the living. Why do you pass judgment on your brother? Or why do you despise your brother?" (Rom. 14:7-9). We must therefore "let all bitterness and wrath and anger and clamor and slander be put away, with all malice, and be kind to one another, tender hearted, forgiving one another, as God in Christ forgave" us (Eph. 4:31-32; cf. also Phil. 2:1-4; Col. 3:8-15). We must "to that end keep alert with all perseverance, making supplication for all the saints" (Eph 6:18).

The fact that we form one body with Christ is supremely revealed, verified and experienced, in the time between the ascension of Christ and his second coming, in the celebration of the Eucharist. When baptized Christians gather round the bread and the wine, over which the dedicated "minister of the word" has pronounced the Eucharist or thanksgiving, and receive the body and blood of Christ in the gifts thus sanctified, they are then the Body of Christ, and are made still more the Body of Christ by their continued reception of the Eucharist. "The cup of blessing which we bless, is it not a participation in the blood of Christ? The bread which we break, is it not a participation in the body of Christ? Because there is one bread, we who are many are one body, for we all partake of the one bread" (1 Cor. 10:16-17).

The Lord, sitting on the right hand of the Father, communicates himself to the Church in the eucharistic event. He himself is present in the community of the Church when it gives thanks to the Father in this event, so that thanks are given by both the Head and the members of the body, in other words, by the "whole Christ." He is with his own in his Spirit, who inspires the prayer of thanks in their hearts and gives it power with the Father. He is with his own in his servant, the one who holds office in the community and has to speak and act "in the name of Jesus." Finally, he is the thanksgiving itself, under the signs of bread and wine, in which he dedicates himself wholly to the Father for the forgiveness of the sins of the many.

The eucharistic bread is the body of the Lord, and the wine of the Eucharist is his blood. The Lord is, according to his own words, "the living bread which came down from heaven: if any one eats of this bread, he will live for ever; and the bread which I shall give for the life of the world is my flesh." Jesus went on to amplify this statement: "For my flesh is food indeed, and my blood is drink indeed. He who eats my flesh and drinks my blood abides in me, and I in him. . . . As I live because of the Father, so he who eats me will live because of me" (John 6:51-57). Both John and Paul made use of this profound formulation of Christian unity — he is in us, and we are in him. In this connection, the evangelist reproduced Jesus' parable of the vine and the branches — the branches live in the vine and the vine lives and is active in the branches. The apostle, on the other hand, refers to the members living in the body and the body living in its members. This state of being in each other is brought to fulfillment by Jesus in the celebration of the Eucharist. In the words of his dedicated servant, the Lord says to his own: "Take and eat all of you of this, for this is my body; take and drink all of you of this, for this is the chalice of my blood." Those who are gathered around come forward and receive the body of Christ, and this action does not cause "the body of Christ to be changed in them, but they are changed into the body of Christ" (Augustine). The celebration of the Eucharist is therefore the constant point of departure for the existence of the Church as the body of Christ and an activity to which it is always committed, for the body of Christ, which is the Church, cannot exist without the eucharistic body of Christ. In Jesus' own words, "unless you eat the flesh of the Son of man and drink his blood, you have no life in you" (John 6:53).

Every Christian who shares in the Eucharist finds fellowship with his Lord, as the one who is the Head of the body and who gives himself "for many" (Mark 14:24). The eucharistic bread is one and it is for this reason that "we who are many are one body" (1 Cor. 10:17). This comparison was further elaborated in connection with the bread in the earliest document of the Church that we possess after the Bible: "Just as this bread, which we are about to break, made of grains of corn previously scattered on the fields, and just as this wine, pressed from grapes previously dispersed over the hills, were gathered and are now lying together on thy table, assemble, Lord, like them, the whole of thy Church from the ends of the earth" (Didache, Chapter 9). Augustine and Thomas Aquinas linked this comparison with the Pauline image of 1 Cor. 10:16-17: "The Church is called the one bread and the one body because, 'just as one loaf is composed of many grains of corn and one body of many members, so too is the Church of Christ composed of many faithful, bound together by love."

The bond between the Eucharist and the people of God was expressed for the community of the New Testament by adopting the Greek term **ekklesia** from the Old Covenant. The first idea that was called to mind by the word **ekklesia** in the situation of the Old Testament was that of the community assembled during worship. The second idea was that of the people of God as such. The New Testament meaning of **ekklesia** is firstly the community, either of a household or of a city, assembled at the celebration of the Eucharist, and secondly the Church as a whole. The universal Church is represented, or thought of as being present, in the community celebrating the Eucharist. In other words, the Eucharist is the place where the universal unity of the Church appears and is present.

In the Passover, the Jews celebrated the grace of their fellowship with God, their belief that they were the one people of God by virtue of the one Covenant. Jesus instituted the New Covenant in the context of this feast of the Old Covenant and the Eucharist as the Church's Passover. God thus established a New Covenant in Christ's blood and in this way fashioned a new people for himself, a new people of God which was open to receive all men. Just as the plan of salvation before the coming of Christ had been accomplished in one Covenant and one people, so were the fulfillment of this plan and the Eucharist the moment at which not only the "New Covenant in my Blood" but also the new people of God became a living reality. The Lord gave the "cup of the New Covenant in my Blood" (Luke 22:20) to the disciples to drink at the Last Supper as the first fruits of the new people, and every time that the Eucharist is celebrated, the beginning of the Eucharist, in the Lord's Supper in the upper room, is made present and the unity of the new people of God becomes increasingly real.[15]

With this idea in mind, the Eastern Church prays: "Sharing in the one bread and the one chalice, we are all one with each other in communion with the one Holy Spirit" (The liturgy of Basil). The Western Church too prays: "Be gracious, Lord, to your Church and grant her the gifts of unity and peace, which are shown in a symbolic manner under the gifts offered here" (Prayer over the offering, the feast of Corpus Christi). The eucharistic celebration is therefore the proper time and place for the constant preservation and the further building up of the body of Christ. This is the task both of individual believers, who must become more and more members of the body of Christ, and of the Church as a whole, which is still on the way to the time when "we all attain to the unity of the faith and of the knowledge of the Son of God, to mature manhood, to the measure of the stature of the fullness of Christ" (Eph. 4:13).

The Eucharist is the sign and the source of the unity of the Church, but it is at the same time the most painfully obvious moment of Christian disunity in the life of the Church. Whenever Catholics gather round the Lord's table in their own parish, they celebrate the Eucharist in mutual fellowship, and also "together with your servant, our Pope N., and our bishop N., and with all those who truly believe and practice the Catholic and apostolic faith" (Canon of the Mass according to the Roman rite). This unity of the local community and the universal Church is also the visible sign of the frontier set up between the Catholics and the other Christians of that district and all the other Christian communities who are not in full communion with the college of bishops gathered around the office of Peter. Yet these separated Christians are baptized, and "through baptism we share in the unity of the Church, of which unity the Eucharist is the sacrament" (Thomas Aquinas). These other baptized Christians cannot, in conscience, take part in the Catholic celebration of the Eucharist, which is an expression of the Catholic confession of faith. We are also not able, for the same reason, simply to invite them to take part. Yet they are baptized into the body of Christ, the eucharistic and ecclesiastical body of the Lord. That they cannot

in fact attain to this full fellowship must inevitably
fill both us and them with sadness and anxiety. The
fact that so many baptized Christians are absent
from our celebration of the Eucharist means that
its joy is incomplete. The reasons why not all Christians are present at our eucharistic celebration are
to be found not only on their side, but also on our
own, and the fact of our separation should serve to
remind us of St. Paul's warning: "I appeal to you,
brethren, by the name of our Lord Jesus Christ, that
all of you agree and that there be no dissension
among you, but that you be united in the same
mind and the same judgment. . . . Is Christ divided?"
(1 Cor. 1:10, 13). Christ cannot be divided, but the
unity of his body, the Church, has been deprived
of much of its luster and fullness. Whenever we
celebrate the Eucharist and see Christ's body on
the table, the body that we too are, we are inevitably
saddened because of our absent brethren and reminded of them in the prayer of the canon and of
preparation for communion, that the Lord may
"grant his Church peace and unity in accordance
with his will."[16]

The full unity for which we pray and which we
expect from the Lord of the Church will be given
to us according to the measure in which all baptized
Christians, both inside and outside the Catholic
Church, become more fully members of Christ. We
shall approach each other more closely according to
the measure in which all of us "grow up in every
way into him who is the Head, into Christ" (Eph.

4:15), and in this way the body will "make growth and upbuild itself in love" (Eph. 4:16). It is not we who shall make peace among ourselves, but those who receive him who is "our peace" and who "came and preached peace to those who were far off and peace to those who were near; for through him we both have access in one Spirit to the Father" (Eph. 2:14, 17-18).

CONCLUSION

The Bible, God's book, occupies a central position in the community, on the altar and in the pulpit, in Catholic, Orthodox and Reformed churches. In the center of each individual Christian group, and central among the separated Christian communities, it testifies to the grace of God's all-embracing initiative to bring reconciliation, "to unite all things to him (Christ), things in heaven and things on earth" (Eph. 1:10).

This divine testimony of reconciliation reveals the origin, the means brought about by God and the aim of this universal unity in Christ. It also instructs and consoles us by providing us with the history of the way in which God has caused this unity to come about among us, from its earliest beginning in the man Abraham to its ultimate completion in the "great multitude which no man could number, from every nation, from all tribes and peoples and tongues" (Apoc. 7:9).

God himself is the **origin** of this universal unity. The "We" of the Father, the Word and the Spirit, who live from, with and in one another, is the source, inaccessible to us, of this unity. As the Three in One, they experience a perfect unity in active and loving intercommunication and in joyous peace.

This mystery of the life of the three Persons in the perfect and joyous unity of the one Trinity was revealed to mankind so that men too might have "life and peace" and "peace and joy" (Rom. 8:6; 14:17). It found its resting-point on its journey to man in the incarnation of the Word: "In the beginning was the Word, and the Word was with God, and the Word was God. He was in the beginning with God; all things were made through him, . . . and the Word became flesh and dwelt among us, full of grace and truth; we have beheld his glory, glory as of the only Son from the Father. . . . And from his fullness have we all received" (John 1:1-2, 14, 16). The source of this divine mystery on earth is Jesus Christ, "through whom are all things and through whom we exist" (1 Cor. 8:6). He communicates the mystery to us through the one Holy Spirit, who "has been given to us" and who "really dwells in" us (Rom. 5:5; 8:9). He is the "Spirit of Christ" the Son and makes us the adopted sons of the Father and brothers and fellow heirs" of Christ (Rom. 8:9, 17). The fruits of the Spirit in us are also a reflection of and our share, as creatures, in the life, peace and joy of God.

The **means** which God provides so that this one life may be revealed to us and so that we may be able really to share in it are the one gospel (Gal. 1:7), the one baptism, by which we are incorporated into Christ's Body (Eph. 4:5) and the one Eucharist, by which the life of Christ's Body, the Church, is preserved (1 Cor. 10:17).

These three effective signs of salvation are maintained in an uninterrupted sequence by the apostolic office and encircled by various charismatic gifts, through which the one Spirit of the Lord is "for ever" active (1 Cor. 12:4-11; John 14:16).

We, for our part, should accept this invitation to union with God and with each other in the one Christ by accepting God's gift to us, that is, by being positive and receptive in our attitude towards the three signs of salvation and by being ready to listen to those who have been appointed by God to administer these signs. If we do this, God will indeed make us one, establishing with bonds of faith, hope and love a unity which we, gathered round the Word and the sacrament, shall experience both inwardly and outwardly, "with all lowliness and meekness, with patience, forbearing one another in love" (Eph. 4:1-6).

The **aim** of unity in Christ is the return of all men to God's home, the Church, whom "Christ loved" and for whom "he gave himself up . . . that he might sanctify her, having cleansed her by the washing of water with the Word, that he might present the Church to himself in splendor, without spot or wrinkle or any such thing, that she might be holy and without blemish" (Eph. 5:25-27). It is then that the Church will be fully the Lord's, and full of God's glory.

"I saw the holy city, new Jerusalem, coming down out of heaven from God, prepared as a bride adorned

for her husband; and I heard a great voice from the
throne saying, 'Behold, the dwelling of God is with
men. He will dwell with them, and they shall be
his people, and God himself will be with them;
he will wipe away every tear from their eyes, and
death shall be no more, neither shall there be
mourning nor crying nor pain any more, for the
former things have passed away.' And he who sat
upon the throne said, 'Behold, I will make all things
new . . . It is done! I am the Alpha and the Omega,
the beginning and the end' " (Rev. 21:2-6).

The apostle John, who took part in the foundation
of the Church and in her history for several decades
after the ascension of the Lord, was permitted to
behold this completion in a vision. He was granted
a vision of "the Bride, the wife of the Lamb" (Rev.
21:9) at a time when the Church was failing to make
ancient Israel as a whole follow her vocation in the
new phase of her existence and when the Church
was suffering from inner tensions and had even
perhaps experienced her first division (3 John 9).

"The holy city Jerusalem coming down out of
heaven from God, having the glory of God . . . It
had a great, high wall, with twelve gates, . . . and on
the gates the names of the twelve tribes of the sons
of Israel were inscribed . . . And the wall of the
city had twelve foundations, and on them the twelve
names of the twelve apostles of the Lamb . . . The
wall was built of jasper, while the city was pure
gold, clear as glass. The foundations of the wall of
the city were adorned with every jewel . . . And

the twelve gates were twelve pearls, each of the
gates made of a single pearl, and the street of the
city was pure gold, transparent as glass. And I saw
no temple in the city, for its temple is the Lord God
the Almighty and the Lamb. And the city has no
need of sun or moon to shine upon it, for the glory
of God is its light, and its lamp is the Lamb. By its
light shall the nations walk" (Rev. 21:10-24).

John prophesied that the servants "of God and of
the Lamb" would enter this city and "see his face"
(Rev. 22:3, 4). The multitude would stand before
him, whose life was their origin and whose presence
was their joy. They would "see him as he is" (1
John 3:2), "face to face" (1 Cor. 13:12). This happiness
filled the heavenly Church with "the mighty voice of
a great multitude," "a voice . . . like the sound of
many waters and like the sound of loud thunder;
the voice . . . was like the sound of harpers playing
on their harps, and they sing a new song before the
throne . . . No one could learn that song except they"
(Rev. 19:1; 14:2-3).

We are called to this one song of praise, made
with one voice, one heart and one soul. Indeed,
we are moving towards the point where we shall
sing it together. This vision of the heavenly Church,
of the united and singleminded "followers of the
Lamb," has been recorded for us who still have
difficulty in following "the Lamb wherever he goes"
(Rev. 14:4) and do not always succeed in being
one flock. This vision, which may seem to us still
to be very distant, has been explicitly confirmed by

God: "These words are trustworthy and true . . . Blessed is he who keeps the words of the prophecy of this book" (Rev. 22:6-7). We shall indeed be surprised when we see the fulfillment of this prophecy and have fellowship with those who belong to the churches of the West and of the East and with the saints whom we have forgotten — the saints of Jerusalem and Antioch, Alexandria and Constantinople, of holy Russia and the Church of England, of the Lutheran and Reformed churches and of the various movements and missions — and with the many people "who have borne witness for Christ, sometimes even by shedding their blood," as the Second Vatican Council has expressed it.

Now, however, we are still involved in the history through which God plans to accomplish in us the mystery of our becoming one. This history is, as far as God is concerned, always a clear and straightforward process, but we frequently resist the fulfillment of God's plan in it. While he is leading us towards unity, we often tend towards disunity. The landmarks which God has set up to guide us on our journey through this history towards the goal of universal reconciliation are clear and immovable — Abraham, Israel, Jesus Christ, the apostolic community, the one baptism, the one Eucharist and the one city. The Church's pilgrimage along the road marked by these milestones has always been accompanied by differences of opinion, intolerance and a half-hearted and hesitant response to God's leadership.

God's Spirit, however, has always caused so many to listen to the Word of God that the divine call to unity is never completely silenced, but is always heard in its true form in our divided world. Because God is faithful, his people will always be present in the world. Because Christ died and was glorified by the Father, his body, the Church, will never perish. We believe in the holy unity of the apostolic Church as an imperishable gift which the glorified Lord, who is our living Head ever present with the Father, never ceases to bestow upon his Body. It is he who preserves his Bride and her indivisible heart, that is always "anxious about the affairs of the Lord, how to please the Lord, . . . how to be holy in body and spirit" (1 Cor. 7:32-34).

It is the Book of Reconciliation itself, always central in the Church, that reassures us in this belief. What is seemingly impossible to men — the fact that so many Christians, from so many different nations and civilizations, of such diverse human types and at such various periods of history, have always been and are still brought together and kept together — is possible with God. God's testimony of this in the Bible is not only an instruction for our encouragement and a warning based on experience; it is also in itself a power — what God says, is!

The Book of divine unity is also, however, a testimony against us whenever we resist the voice of the one Shepherd. Those who believe are called "saints" in the Bible, but are at the same time constantly urged to an unceasing conversion from their sinfulness. In the same way, God's Church is one, but is at the same time continuously urged to put away all temptation to disunity, all quarrelling, jealousy and ambition and all lack of truth and love.

The Book of unity is an unceasing call to Catholics to become more and more fully one. In a Church whose members — people of such widely differing temperaments — are to be found all over the world in so many different societies, it sometimes seems very difficult to produce a truly common evaluation of all the various rites, regulations, traditions and pious practices and of the proper responsibilities and powers of the local churches. The separate parishes and institutions, organizations and associations within each diocese are often very reluctant to show tolerance or to sacrifice anything for the sake of the diocese or the Church as a whole. Even within individual parishes, religious communities, lay associations and parish guilds and confraternities, there is frequently only very limited cooperation, little mutual tolerance and forgiveness and little sympathy for brothers within the group and for all brethren in Christ. Any lack of brotherly love within the Church is a sin against the Lord himself. It is a cause of scandal to weaker brethren. It is also the cause of the offence quoted by St. Paul: "The name of God is blasphemed among the Gentiles because of you" (Rom. 2:24). The Book of Reconciliation has this to say on the subject of giving scandal: "Give no offence to Jews or to Greeks or to the church of God, just as I (Paul) try to please all men in everything I do, not seeking my own advantage, but that of many, that they may be saved. Be imitators of me, as I am of Christ" (1 Cor. 10:32; 11:1).

The growth of love and truth within the Church will also result in Catholic unity becoming better fitted once again to receive those baptized Christians who have themselves left her, or whose forefathers have left her. This will not only be a question of a return of separated Christians to the concrete and historical Catholic unity, but of a renewal of our unity, so that we grow together with our separated brethren towards a divine maturity, a "growth that is from God" (Col. 2:19). If we and our separated brethren allow ourselves to be renewed by the Spirit and the words of God's Book, we shall together find ways of experiencing once again the unity of Christ's Body, of giving the Lord the perfect luster of his body in the celebration of the one Eucharist and finally of removing from the world the scandal of a divided Christianity.

It is clear from the increasing alarm, both in the Catholic Church and outside her, concerning the divided state of Christianity, that the Holy Spirit and the testimony of Holy Scripture are making themselves felt more strongly at the present time than in the past. The Christian world is moving today towards unity, and not only Christian pastors and teachers, but also more and more of the faithful are becoming increasingly aware of their responsibility for the inadmissible situation in which Christians have been placed in the world today. The most hopeful aspect of this comprehensive modern movement is the irresistible urge on the part of so many, even those who live in obscurity, to say, together with the Lord of all Christians, his own prayer for unity: "Father, that they may all be one" (John 17:21). And the Spirit of Christian unity would not evoke this prayer in us if he did not mean to give us what he makes us ask.

NOTES

1. *Begegnung der Christen,* ed. M. Roesle and O. Cull-mann, Stuttgart and Frankfurt am Main (1960), p. 83.

2. L. Cerfaux, *La théologie de l'église suivant saint Paul,* Paris (1948²) p. 122, note p. 32-47.

3. Decree on Ecumenism, no. 3.

4. Decree on Ecumenism, no. 4.

5. J. van der Ploeg, *Vondsten in de woestijn van Juda; de rollen der Dode Zee,* Utrecht (1957).

6. J. Ratzinger, *Die christliche Brüderlichkeit,* Munich (1960).

7. D. Deden, *De Bijbel over de Kerk,* Roermond and Maaseik (1962).

8. L. Cerfaux, *op. cit.,* pp. 150, 139.

9. F. M. Braun, *Neues Licht auf die Kirche,* Einsiedeln (1946), p. 71.

10. P. Gaechter, *Petrus und seine Zeit; neutestamentliche Studien,* Innsbruck (1958), pp. 36-38.

11. P. Gaechter, *op. cit.,* pp. 22-30.

12. K. H. Schelkle, *Jüngerschaft und Apostelamt,* Freiburg (1957), p. 44.

13. M. Villain, *La priére de Jésus pour l'unité chrétienne; méditation oecuménique sur Jean XVII,* Tournai (1960); W. Thüsing, *Herrlichkeit und Einheit; eine Auslegung des Hohepriesterlichen Gebets Johannes 17,* Düsseldorf (1962).

14. O. Cullmann, *Katholiken und Protestanten,* Basle (1958); P. Drijvers, *Wat de jonge Kerk ons te zeggen heeft; beschouwingen bij Handelingen 1-13,* Utrecht (1960).

15. P. Blaser. *"Eucharistie und Einheit der Kirche in der Verkündigung des Neuen Testaments,"* Theologie und Glaube 50 (1960), pp. 419-432.

16. J. Lescrauwaet, *"Eucharistische eredienst en kerkelijke eenheid,"* Bijdragen 25 (1964), pp. 117-142.